KU-330-797

An atlas is a book of maps. The maps in the first part of this atlas tell you about the United Kingdom. The other maps tell you about the continents. Some of the maps focus on themes or topics. There is an index at the back to help you find where places are.

Most of maps in this atlas are about people and their surroundings. For example, you can find out where people live, how they travel from place to place and about the plants and scenery in different parts of the world. Photographs, charts and diagrams provide extra information. There are files with lots of interesting facts.

Atlas makers have to make many choices. They have to decide which places to include and which places to leave out. It's impossible to show everything. They also try to choose things which you will find interesting. Each page is full of information.

Our world never stays the same. This atlas tells you about the world today. The choices that people make will change the world in the years to come. Thinking about the future reminds us that the Earth is the only home we have.

Editorial advisor Dr. Stephen Scoffham is the Honorary Publications Officer of the Geographical Association

The Geographical Association exists to further the study, learning and teaching of geography. Founded in 1893, it is one of the UK's leading subject associations and membership is open to any person or body of people interested in supporting its core objectives. This atlas, one of a range of resources for primary and secondary schools available from the Geographical Association, is published in conjunction with Collins. Further details about the Association and its work are available at www.geography.org.uk

COLLINS JUNIOR WORLD ATLAS
Collins
An imprint of HarperCollins Publishers
77-85 Fulham Palace Road, London W6 8JB

© HarperCollins Publishers 2011
Maps © Collins Bartholomew Ltd 2011

First published 2009, reprinted 2009, 2010. Second edition 2011

This edition produced for The Book People Ltd, Parc Menai, Bangor LL57 4FB

ISBN 978 0 00 789289 1

Imp 001

IN ASSOCIATION WITH

Collins   Geographical Association

Collins ® is a registered trademark of HarperCollins Publishers Ltd

All rights reserved. No part of this publication may be reproduced, stored in a retrieval system, or transmitted in any form or by any means, electronic, mechanical, photocopying, recording or otherwise, without the prior written permission of the publisher or copyright owners.

The contents of this edition of the Collins Junior World Atlas are believed correct at the time of printing. Nevertheless the publishers can accept no responsibility for errors or omissions, changes in the detail given, or for any expense or loss thereby caused.

British Library Cataloguing in Publication Data
A catalogue record for this book is available from the British Library.

Printed and bound in Hong Kong

All mapping in this atlas is generated from Collins Bartholomew digital databases. Collins Bartholomew, the UK's leading independent geographical information supplier, can provide a digital, custom, and premium mapping service to a variety of markets. For further information:
Tel: +44 (0) 141 306 3752
e-mail: collinsbartholomew@harpercollins.co.uk
Visit our websites at:
www.collinseducation.com
www.collinsbartholomew.com
www.collinsmaps.com

Collins Junior World Atlas

Editorial advisor **Dr. Stephen Scoffham**

Contents

2 What is an atlas?

Globes

Globes are models of the earth. They show the true shape and size of the continents.

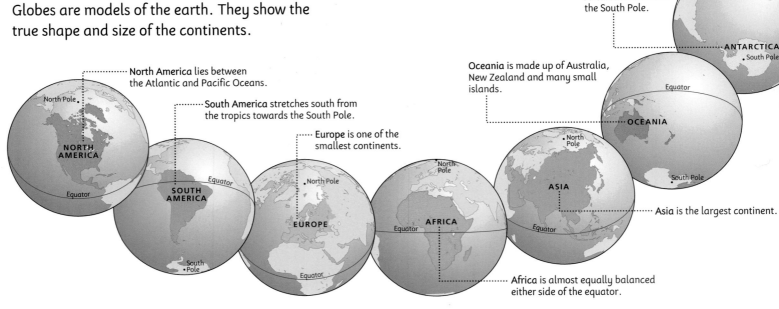

North America lies between the Atlantic and Pacific Oceans.

South America stretches south from the tropics towards the South Pole.

Europe is one of the smallest continents.

Africa is almost equally balanced either side of the equator.

Antarctica encircles the South Pole.

Oceania is made up of Australia, New Zealand and many small islands.

Asia is the largest continent.

Mapping the world

To show the world on a flat map we need to peel the surface of the globe and flatten it out. There are many different methods of drawing atlas maps. These methods are called **projections**.

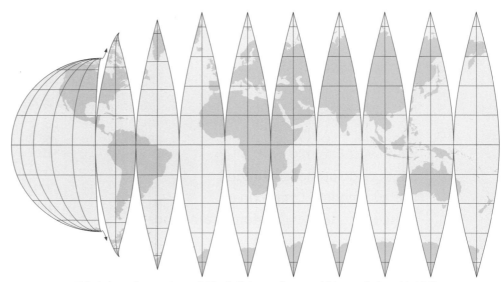

This is how the earth would look if the surface could be peeled and laid flat.

Projections

Map projections change the shape and size of the continents and oceans. The projection used for world maps in this atlas is called Eckert IV.

How the world map looks, depends on which continents are at the centre of the map. Compare the shape of Africa on the maps below to that on the globe.

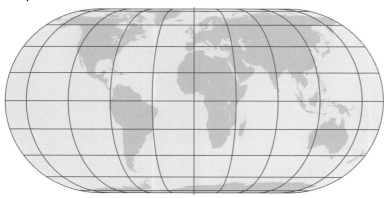

For UK atlases the world would look like this.

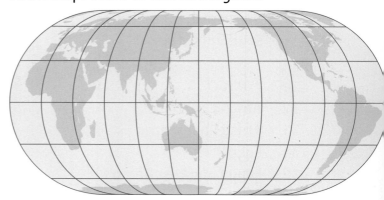

For Australian atlases the world would look like this.

Latitude and longitude

We use latitude and longitude to locate places on the earth's surface. Lines of **latitude** are imaginary lines. They are numbered in degrees North or South of the equator. Lines of **longitude** are imaginary lines which run from the North to the South Poles. They are numbered in degrees East or West of a line through London known as the Prime Meridian.

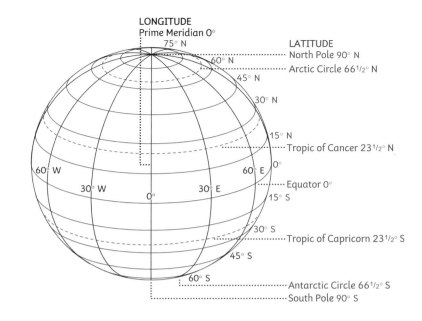

Grid references

Lines of latitude and longitude are used in this atlas to make a grid. The columns are labelled with a letter and the rows with a number. The grid code e.g. B6 can be used to find all places within one grid square.

Cartagena is in B8

Bogota is in B7

Piura is in A6

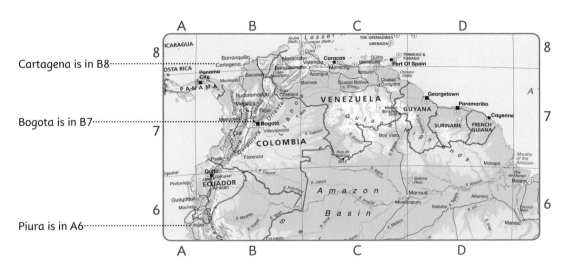

Hemispheres

The equator divides the globe into two halves. All land north of the equator is called the northern hemisphere. Land south of the equator is called the southern hemisphere. 0° and 180° lines of longitude also divide the globes into two imaginary halves, the western and eastern hemispheres.

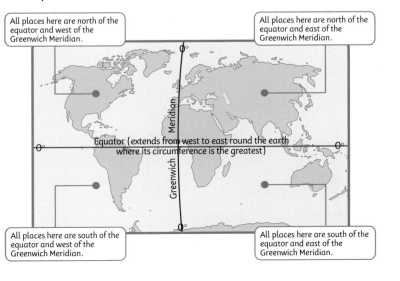

All places here are north of the equator and west of the Greenwich Meridian.

All places here are north of the equator and east of the Greenwich Meridian.

Equator (extends from west to east round the earth where its circumference is the greatest)

Greenwich Meridian

All places here are south of the equator and west of the Greenwich Meridian.

All places here are south of the equator and east of the Greenwich Meridian.

Direction

On most atlas maps you will find a compass. It shows the four compass points North (N), East (E), South (S) and West (W). These help us give more accurate directions.

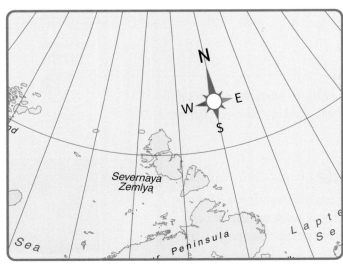

On atlas maps the north point always follows a line of longitude.

4 What is an atlas?

Atlas maps

Atlas maps tell us about the various parts of the world. They tell us about different environments in the world.

Some maps show country shapes and where towns are located within the country. These are called political maps.

Some maps show landscapes. They show the physical environment.

Special names and numbers

Special names and numbers are used to label parts of an atlas map.

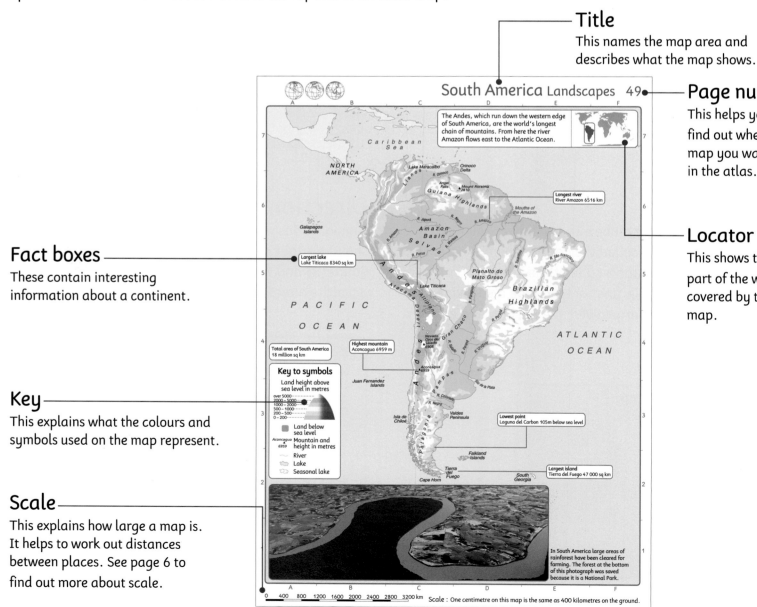

Title
This names the map area and describes what the map shows.

Page number
This helps you to find out where the map you want is in the atlas.

Locator map
This shows the part of the world covered by the map.

Fact boxes
These contain interesting information about a continent.

Key
This explains what the colours and symbols used on the map represent.

Scale
This explains how large a map is. It helps to work out distances between places. See page 6 to find out more about scale.

Map symbols

Maps are made up of symbols and names. The symbols can be points, lines or area colours.
A map is complete when the symbols and the names are combined.

Point symbols

- ■ Town stamps
- ▲ Mountain peaks
- ⊕ Airports

Lines

—— Roads	⊷⊷ Railways
—— Country boundaries	
—— Rivers and canals	
—— Coastline	

Area colours

☐ Lake/sea

Land height above sea level in metres

over 5000 ············
3000 – 5000 ············
2000 – 3000 ············
1000 – 2000 ············
500 – 1000 ············
200 – 500 ············
0 – 200 ············

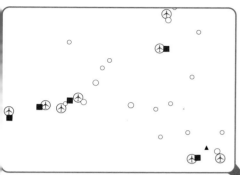

Point symbols are used on a map to show towns, mountain peaks and airports.

Lines are used on a map to show communications and drainage.

Area colours are used to distinguish the land from the sea and land height above sea level.

Names on atlas maps

The style and size of the type used on maps helps to explain what the name means.

Large bodies of water

PACIFIC OCEAN
Gulf of Guinea

Islands

Cuba
Bioco

Countries

NIGERIA
BENIN

Large cities

Porto-Novo
Lomé

Small towns

Parakou
Warri

Rivers

Mississippi
Nile
Amazon

Mountain peaks

Mount Cameroon
Everest

All the symbols are combined to show features and their correct locations.

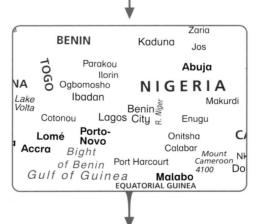

Names are needed to show places and features shown on the map. Only some places and features are named.

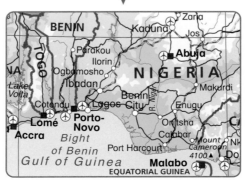

The map is complete when the symbols and the names are combined.

Scale

Maps are much smaller than the regions they show. To
compare the real area with the mapped area you have
to use a scale. Each map in this atlas shows its scale.
This is shown using a scale bar which is explained in words.

E.g.

| 0 | 200 | 400 | 600 | 800 km |

Scale : One centimetre on this map is the same as 200 kilometres on the ground.

Large scale maps
show smaller areas
with more detail.

LARGE SCALE

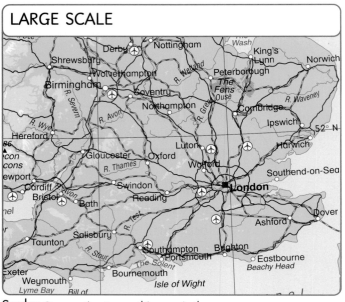

Scale: One centimetre on this map is the same as
40 kilometres on the ground.

| 0 | 40 | 80 | 120 | 160 | 200 km |

MEDIUM SCALE

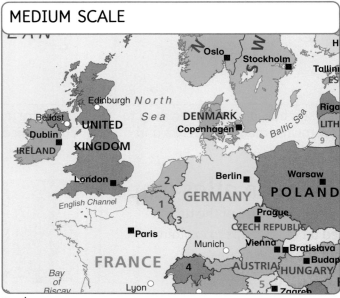

Scale: One centimetre on this map is the same as
250 kilometres on the ground.

| 0 | 250 | 500 | 750 | 1000 | 1250 km |

Measuring distance

The scale of a map can be used to measure how far it is
between two places. For example, the straight line distance
between Boa Vista and Cayenne on the map to the right is
5 centimetres.

Look at the ruler.
One centimetre on this map is the same as 200 kilometres on
the ground. The real distance between Boa Vista and Cayenne
is therefore 1000 kilometres (i.e. 5 X 200).

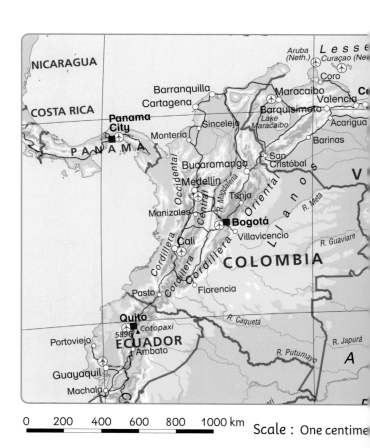

| 0 | 200 | 400 | 600 | 800 | 1000 km |

Scale : One centime

Extend your knowledge and understanding by visiting these websites which provide lots of information and material to help with your homework and projects.

Places

European Union europa.eu/abc/
CIA Factbook www.cia.gov/cia/publications/factbook
Visit Britain www.visitbritain.com
Kids web Japan web-japan.org/kidsweb

Climate

Weather in the UK and abroad www.bbc.co.uk/weather
World climate statistics www.worldclimate.com
Climate change www.greenpeace.org.uk/climate

Population

World Population Prospects esa.un.org/unpp

Geography

National Geographic kids.nationalgeographic.com
Royal Geographical Society www.rgs.org

Mountains and rivers

Mountains of the world www.peakware.com
Rivers and coasts www.bbc.co.uk/schools/riversandcoasts

Maps and satellite images

Google Earth www.google.com/earth
Earth Observatory earthobservatory.nasa.gov
Ordnance Survey mapzone.ordnancesurvey.co.uk

International organizations

United Nations www.cyberschoolbus.un.org
The Commonwealth www.youngcommonwealth.org
Oxfam www.oxfam.org.uk/coolplanet/kidsweb
ActionAid International www.actionaid.org
Christian Aid www.christianaid.org.uk/resources/games
UNICEF www.unicef.org
Save the Children www.savethechildren.org

Environment

Greenpeace www.greenpeace.org.uk
World Wide Fund for Nature www.wwf.org.uk
Fairtrade www.fairtrade.org.uk
Recyclezone www.recyclezone.org.uk
Eco Friendly Kids www.ecofriendlykids.co.uk

Small scale maps show larger areas with less detail.

SMALL SCALE

Scale: One centimetre on this map is the same as 800 kilometres on the ground.

0   800   1600 2400 3200 km

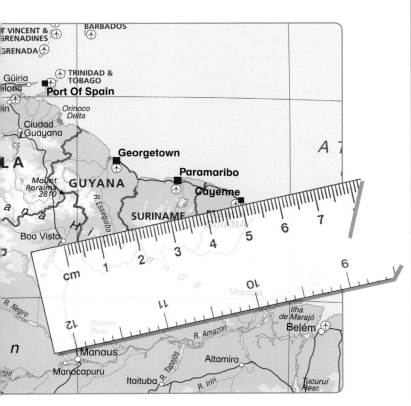

ap is the same as 200 kilometres on the ground.

The islands to the northwest of mainland Europe are divided between two countries – the United Kingdom and Ireland. The largest island, called Great Britain, is the eighth largest in the world.

Shetland Islands
Mainland
Lerwick
Sumburgh Head
Fair Isle

Key to symbols

- ■ Capital city
- ○ Main city/town
- ○ Other city/town
- ▬ Country boundary
- — Road
- ⊢ Railway
- ✈ Airport
- Lake
- ～ River
- Ben Nevis ▲ 1344 Mountain and height in metres

Land height above sea level in metres

- over 5000
- 3000 – 5000
- 2000 – 3000
- 1000 – 2000
- 500 – 1000
- 200 – 500
- 0 – 200

Land below sea level

ATLANTIC OCEAN

UNITED KINGDOM

IRELAND

North Sea

Irish Sea

North Channel

St George's Channel

Celtic Sea

English Channel

Orkney Islands, Mainland, Hoy, Kirkwall, Pentland Firth, Duncansby Head, Thurso, Wick, Fair Isle
Cape Wrath, Butt of Lewis, Isle of Lewis, Stornoway, The Minch, Harris, Tarbert, St Kilda, North Uist, Uig, Skye, South Uist, Outer Hebrides
Loch Shin, Ullapool, Loch Ness, Moray Firth, Inverness, R. Spey, Rattray Head
Cairngorm Mts, Ben Macdui 1309, R. Dee, R. Don, Aberdeen
North West Highlands, Grampian Mountains, Ben Nevis 1344, Fort William, Rum, Coll, Tiree, Inner Hebrides, Mull, Oban, Firth of Lorn, Jura, Islay
Ben More 1174, Loch Tay, Loch Lomond, R. Tay, Perth, Dundee, Firth of Tay
R. Forth, Stirling, Firth of Forth, Glasgow, Edinburgh, Berwick-upon-Tweed
R. Clyde, Firth of Clyde, Ayr, R. Tweed, Cheviot Hills
Arran, Mull of Kintyre, Merrick 843, Southern Uplands, R. Nith, Dumfries, Newcastle upon Tyne, Sunderland
Stranraer, Solway Firth, Carlisle, R. Tyne, Middlesbrough
Workington, Scafell Pike 977, Lake District, Darlington, R. Tees, North York Moors, Scarborough
Malin Head, Errigal 752, Londonderry, Coleraine, Antrim Hills, Larne, R. Bann, Lough Neagh, Belfast
Donegal, Foyle, Lower Lough Erne, Enniskillen, Upper Lough Erne, Newry, Mourne Mts, Slieve Donard 852
Donegal Bay, Ballina, Sligo, Dundalk, Dundalk Bay, Isle of Man, Douglas, Morecambe Bay, R. Derwent, Flamborough Head
Achill Island, Lough Conn, Westport, Lough Mask, Lough Corrib, Drogheda, Blackpool, Preston, R. Ribble, Bradford, Leeds, York, Kingston upon Hull, Spurn Head
Galway, Galway Bay, Lough Ree, R. Boyle, R. Shannon, Dublin, Liverpool, R. Mersey, Manchester, Huddersfield, Grimsby
Lough Derg, R. Suck, R. Liffey, Anglesey, Holyhead, Chester, Stoke-on-Trent, Sheffield, Doncaster, Lincoln
R. Barrow, R. Nore, Wicklow Mts, Wicklow, Wicklow Head, Caernarfon, Snowdon 1085, Crewe, Derby, Nottingham, R. Trent, The Wash
Limerick, R. Shannon, R. Suir, R. Dee, Cambrian Mountains, Shrewsbury, Wolverhampton, King's Lynn, Peterborough
Tralee, R. Blackwater, Waterford, Wexford, Rosslare, Cardigan Bay, Aberystwyth, Birmingham, Coventry, Northampton, The Fens, R. Welland, R. Great Ouse, R. Waveney, Norwich
Carrantuohill 1041, R. Lee, Cork, Fishguard, St David's Head, Pembroke, Hereford, R. Wye, Gloucester, R. Avon, Cambridge, Ipswich
Cape Clear, Swansea, Brecon Beacons 886, Newport, Cardiff, Bristol, Bath, R. Thames, Oxford, Luton, Watford, Harwich, Southend-on-Sea
Bristol Channel, Exmoor, R. Severn, Swindon, Reading, London
Penzance, Land's End, Isles of Scilly, Lizard Point, Bodmin Moor, Dartmoor 619, R. Tamar, Exeter, R. Exe, Taunton, Salisbury, R. Test, R. Stour, Southampton, Portsmouth, The Solent, Brighton, Eastbourne, Beachy Head
Plymouth, Weymouth, Lyme Bay, Bill of Portland, Bournemouth, Isle of Wight, Ashford
Dieppe, FRANCE

Scale : One centimetre on this map is the same as 40 kilometres on the ground.

0 50 100 150 200 250 300 km

Four countries make up the United Kingdom or UK. They are England, Scotland, Wales and Northern Ireland. The Isle of Man and Channel Islands are also part of the UK but have their own laws.

Key to symbols

- ◣ Countries
- ■ Capital city
- ● National capital
- ○ Important city/town

United Kingdom

Scotland

Northern Ireland

Wales

England

Ireland

Shetland Islands

Orkney Islands

Outer Hebrides

ATLANTIC OCEAN

SCOTLAND

Inverness

Aberdeen

Fort William

Dundee

Glasgow **Edinburgh**

North Sea

Londonderry

NORTHERN IRELAND **Belfast**

IRELAND

Dublin ■

Isle of Man

Irish Sea

Newcastle upon Tyne

Middlesbrough

UNITED

York

Blackpool Bradford Leeds

Preston

Liverpool Manchester Sheffield

KINGDOM

Stoke-on-Trent Derby Nottingham

ENGLAND Norwich

Wolverhampton Leicester

Birmingham Cambridge

WALES Coventry Ipswich

Swansea Oxford

Bristol Reading **London** ■ Southend-on-Sea

Cardiff ●

BELGIUM

Southampton Brighton

Portsmouth

Bournemouth

Plymouth Torquay

Channel Islands

English Channel

FRANCE

The UK government makes laws in the Houses of Parliament in London.

50 100 150 200 250 300 km

Scale : One centimetre on this map is the same as 50 kilometres on the ground.

The Scottish highlands are the emptiest part of the UK. There are many small islands around the coast. They are linked to the mainland by ferry.

Scotland has many mountains. Those which are over 3000 feet (914 m) high are called Munros. This one is in Glen Coe near Ben Nevis.

Key to symbols

- ○ Main city/town
- ○ Other city/town
- — Road
- —|— Railway
- ✈ Airport
- Lake
- River

Ben Nevis ▲ Mountain and
1344 height in metres

Land height above sea level in metres

- over 1500
- 1000 – 1500
- 900 – 1000
- 500 – 900
- 200 – 500
- 100 – 200
- 0 – 100

ATLANTIC OCEAN

Flannan Isles

St Kilda

Outer Hebrides

Scarp

Great Bernera
Loch Langavat

Clishham
799
Tarbert
Harris
Scalpay
Pabbay
Berneray
Rodel
Sound of Harris

Monach Islands

North Uist
Lochmaddy

Benbecula

South Uist
Beinn Mhor
620

Lochboisdale

Eriskay
Sound of Barra
Barra
Sheabhal
383
Vatersay
Castlebay
Sandray

Mingulay

Butt of Lewis
Port of Ness

Tolsta Head

Stornoway
Port Nan Giùran
Eye Peninsula
Lewis
Kebock Head

Scalpay

Rubha Hunish

Little Minch

Loch Snizort
Uig
Dunvegan
Portree
Skye
Cuillin Hills
993 928
Sgurr
Alasdair Blaven
Soay
Canna

Inner Hebrides

Muck

Point of Ardnamurchan
Ben Hogh
104
Arinagour
Coll
Tiree
Scarinish

The Storr
719
Rona
Raasay
Scalpay
Kyle of Lochalsh
Kyleakin

Cuillin Sound

Ardvasar

Rum
Askival
812

Eigg

Sound of Arisaig

Tobermory
Loch Frisa
Lochaline
Morvern

Cape Wrath
Durn
Kinlochbervie
Handa Island
Scourie
Foina
915

Point of Stoer

Lochinver
Loch Assynt
Ben
Ass
99

Summer Isles

Rubha Reidh
Ullapool
Loch Broom
An Teallach
1062
Fionn Loch
Sgurr Mor
1110
WESTER ROSS

Gairloch
Loch Ewe
Loch Maree

L. Torridon
Inner Sound
Sound of Sleat

R. Orrin
Sgurr a'Choi
1083
Loch Monar
Carn Eighe
1183
Glen Affric

Loch Duich
Glen Shiel
Loch Cluanie
Loch Hourn
Ladhar Bheinn
1020
R. Garry
Loch Quoich
Loch Arkaig
Glen Garry

Gulvain
983
Loch Morar
Mallaig
Loch Shiel

Fort William
1344
Sgurr Dhomhnuill
888
Ben Nevis
Loch Leven
Glen Coe
Bidean nam Bian 1150

Loch Sunart
Loch Linnhe
Loch Etive

Sound of Mull

The Minch

0   25   50   75 km

Scale : One centimetre on this map is the same as 12.5 kilometres on the ground.

Main map labels

Fair Isle

Orkney Islands

Papa Westray
Westray
N. Ronaldsay Firth
North Ronaldsay
Eday
Sanday
Rousay
Brough Head
Westray Firth
Stronsay Firth
Stronsay
Loch of Harray
Shapinsay
Stromness
Kirkwall
Mainland
Skaill
Ward Hill 479
Scapa Flow
Hoy
Flotta
Burray
South Ronaldsay
Burwick

59° N

Pentland Firth

Dunnet Head
Thurso B.
John o'Groats
Duncansby Head
Dounreay
Thurso
Loch Watten
Sinclair's Bay
Bettyhill
R. Wick
Wick
Tongue
Loch Loyal
CAITHNESS
Loch Rimsdale
R. Thurso
Lybster
R. Helmsdale
RLAND
Helmsdale
Lairg
R. Brora
Brora
Golspie
Dornoch Firth
Tarbat Ness
Tain
Cromarty Firth
Moray Firth
Black Isle
vergordon
Fortrose
ingwall
onon ridge
Inverness
Moray Firth
R. Ness
R. Nairn
Nairn
Forres
R. Findhorn
Kinloss
Elgin
Lossiemouth
Buckie
Cullen
Banff
Macduff
Fraserburgh
Fochabers
Knock Hill 430
R. Deveron
Crimond
Rattray Head
Turriff
Mintlaw
Peterhead
Rothes
Keith
R. Isla
Dufftown
Huntly
STRATHBOGIE
R. Ythan
Cruden Bay
Oldmeldrum
Ellon
Grantown-on-Spey
Strathspey
Inverurie
R. Don
Kintore
Dyce
Aberdeen
TLAND
Aviemore
Cairn Gorm 1245
R. Avon
Cairngorm Mts
Ben Macdui 1309
Kingussie
ewtonmore
R. Dee
Ballater
Aboyne
R. Dee
Banchory
laith Mountains
Carn nan Gabhar 1121
Braemar
R. Dee
1155
Lochnagar
Stonehaven
North R. Esk
Inverbervie
Glenshee
Dalwhinnie
ampian Mountains
Loch Ericht
Carn Gabhar
Backwater Reservoir
South R. Esk
Laurencekirk
Rannoch
1083
Schiehallion
Loch Tummel
R. Tummel
Blair Atholl
Pitlochry
R. Isla
Brechin
Montrose
Loch
R. Tay
Ben Lawers 1214
R. Lyon
Aberfeldy
Blairgowrie
Coupar Angus
Sidlaw Hills
Kirriemuir
Forfar
Strathmore
Arbroath
Carnoustie

NORTH SEA

Inset map — Shetland Islands

Herma Ness
Unst
Point of Fethaland
Yell Sound
Fetlar
Ronas Hill 450
Yell
Sullom Voe
St. Magnus Bay
Muckle Roe
Toft
Out Skerries
Papa Stour
Mainland
Whalsay
Foula
Lerwick
Bressay
Shetland Islands
60° N
Sumburgh
Sumburgh Head
Fair Isle

58° N

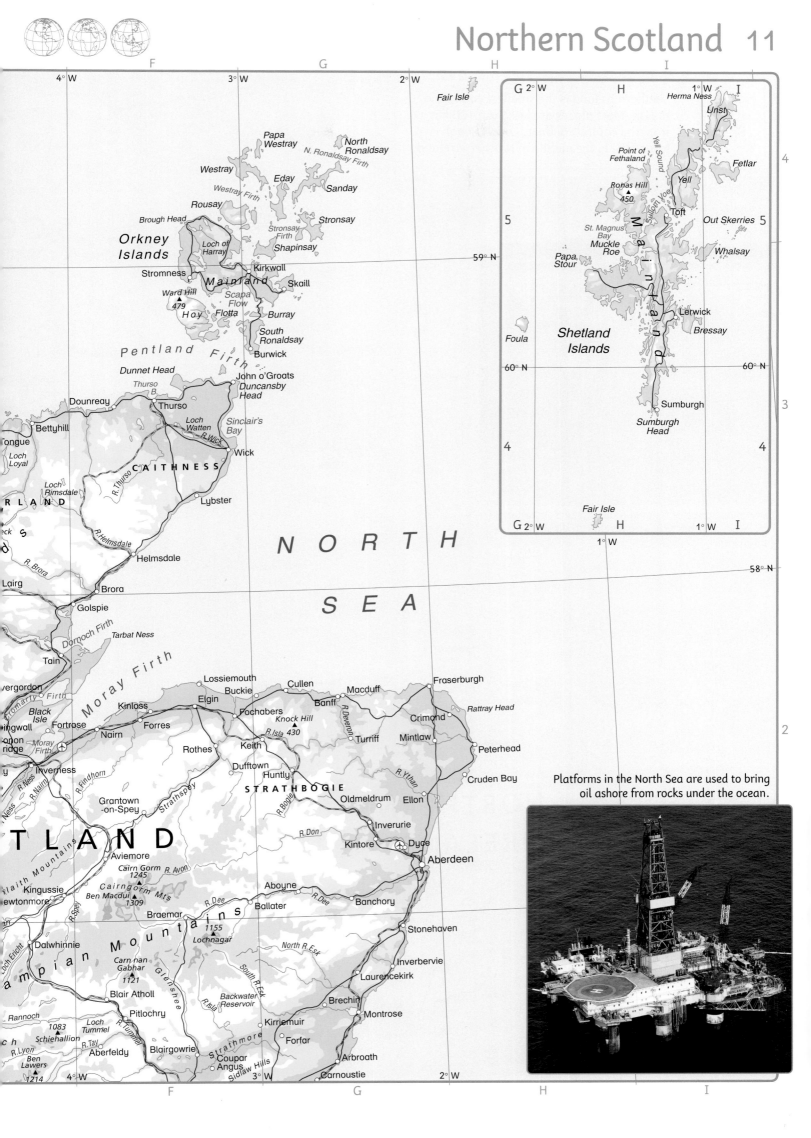

Platforms in the North Sea are used to bring oil ashore from rocks under the ocean.

Northern Ireland is the smallest country in the UK. Most places are less than 100 km from the capital, Belfast. Lough Neagh is a large lake in the middle of Northern Ireland.

After many years of fighting, Catholics and Protestants now work together to govern Northern Ireland from Stormont.

Scale : One centimetre on this map is the same as 12.5 kilometres on the ground.

0   25   50   75 km

SCOTLAND

NORTHERN IRELAND

IRELAND

ISLE OF MAN

IRISH (Sea)

Loch Morar
Gulvain 983
Creag Meagaidh ▲1130
Eigg
Fort William 1344
Ben Alder 1148
Loch Shiel
Sgurr Dhomhnuill 888
Ben Nevis
Muck
Loch Leven
Kintochleven
Glen Coe
Point of Ardnamurchan
Loch Sunart
Morvern
Bidean nam Bian ▲1150
Ben Hogh 104
Arinagour
Tobermory
Lochaline
Coll
Loch Frisa
Sound of Mull
Ben Cruachan 1126
Ben 1130 Crianlarich
Scarinish
Treshnish Isles
Ulva
Ben More 966
Craignure
Mull
Loch Etive
Ben Lui
Tiree
Staffa
Loch Linnhe
Firth of Lorn
Oban
974 Ben Katrine
Iona
Fionnphort
Luing
Loch Awe
Ben Lomond
Loch Long
Lismore
Argyll
Colonsay
Scarba
Sound of Jura
Garelochhead
Helensburgh
Oronsay
Beinn an Oir 785
Lochgilphead
Dunoon
Greenock
Jura
Port Glasgow
Port Askaig
Tarbert
Rothesay
Wemyss Bay
Largs
Paisle
Islay
Kennacraig
Bute
Millport
Great Cumbrae
Bowmore
Gigha
Barrhe
Beinn Bheigeir 491
Kilbrannan Sound
Dalry
Loch Indaal
Port Ellen
Firth of Clyde
Mull Of Oa
Goat Fell 874
Ardrossan
Machrihanish
Arran
Brodick
Irvine
Lamlash
Troon
Rathlin Island
Prestwick
Mull of Kintyre
Ayr
Fair Head
Culzean Bay
Inishtrahull
Malin Head
Giant's Causeway
Ailsa Craig
Girvan
Inishowen
Portrush
Bushmills
Ballycastle
Slieve Snaght 615
Moville
Magilligan Point
Portstewart
Coleraine
R.Bush
Ballantrae
Me 84
Lough Swilly
Buncrana
Lough Foyle
Ballymoney
Trostan 554
Garron Point
Milleur Point
Errigal 752
Derryveagh Mts
Limavady
R.Bann
Antrim Hills
Carnlough
North Channel
Cairnryan
Newton Stewart
Letterkenny
Londonderry
Dungiven
Maghera
Stranraer
R.Foyle
R.Deele
Sawel Mt 683
Sperrin Mts
R.Main
Ballymena
Larne
Wigtown
Lifford
Strabane
Maghera
The Rinns of Galloway
Blue Stack Mts
Blue Stack 676
R.Finn
R.Mourne
Newtownstewart
Magherafelt
Ballyclare
Island Magee
Luce Bay
Lough Eske
Castlederg
Antrim
Carrickfergus
Drummore
Donegal
R.Derg
Cookstown
Lough Neagh
Newtownabbey
Belfast Lough
R.Strule
Omagh
Crumlin
Bangor
Burrow
Lough Derg
Belfast
Newtownards
Dungannon
Lisburn
Comber
Ballyshannon
Strangford Lough
Ards Peninsula
Bundoran
R.Erne
Lurgan
Saintfield
R.Blackwater
Portadown
Craigavon
R.Lagan
Point
Lough Melvin
Lower Lough Erne
Enniskillen
Armagh
Ballynahinch
Banbridge
Portaferry
Tullybrack 376
R.Bann
Manorhamilton
Lisnaskea
Downpatrick
Lough Gill
R.Shannon
Upper Lough Erne
Ulster Canal
Monaghan
Newry
Newcastle
Slieve Donard 852
Ardglass
ISLE OF MAN
Cuncagh 667
Clones
Mourne Mts
Dundrum Bay
Snae 62
Lough Allen
Slieve Anierin 586
Castleblayney
R.Annalee
Warrenpoint
Carlingford L
Peel
Lough Arrow
Lough Key
Lough Oughter
Cavan
Dundalk
Kilkeel
Port Erin
Calf of Man
Castletow
Boyle
Carrick-on-Shannon
Carrickmacross
Dundalk Bay
Ramsc
Lough Boderg
Lough Gowna
Baillieborough
Moyer 341
Kingscourt
Duncalk

8° W   7° W   6° W   5° W
6° W   5° W
56° N
55° N
54° N

Most people in Scotland live in the central lowlands. The biggest cities, Edinburgh and Glasgow, are less than 70 km apart.

Important routes lead north from Edinburgh across the Firth of Forth to other parts of Scotland.

NORTH SEA

ENGLAND

Key to symbols

- ● Country capital
- ○ Main city/town
- ○ Other city/town
- —— Country boundary
- —— Road
- —— Railway
- ⊕ Airport
- Lake
- River
- ▲ Ben Nevis 1344 Mountain and height in metres

Land height above sea level in metres

| over 1500 |
| 1000 – 1500 |
| 900 – 1000 |
| 500 – 900 |
| 200 – 500 |
| 100 – 200 |
| 0 – 100 |

Place names

Lochnagar ▲1155
Carn nan Gabhar ▲1121
Blair Atholl
Pitlochry
Loch Tummel
R. Tummel
R. Tay
Aberfeldy
Blairgowrie
Glenshee
North R. Esk
South R. Esk
R. Isla
Backwater Reservoir
Inverbervie
Laurencekirk
Brechin
Montrose
Kirriemuir
Forfar
Coupar Angus
Strathmore
Sidlaw Hills
Arbroath
Carnoustie
Dundee
Buddon Ness
Tayport
Perth
Crieff
R. Earn
Newburgh
Cupar
Leuchars
St Andrews
Fife Ness
Crail
Anstruther
Pittenweem
Auchterarder
Dunblane
Ochil Hills
Kinross
Falkland
Ladybank
Loch Leven
Markinch
Leven
Dunblane
Tillicoultry
Glenrothes
Kirkcaldy
Alloa
Cowdenbeath
Burntisland
Kincardine
Dunfermline
North Berwick
Grangemouth
Inverkeithing
Firth of Forth
Aberlady
Dunbar
Falkirk
Cumbernauld
Linlithgow
Edinburgh
Musselburgh
Haddington
St Abb's Head
Eyemouth
Bathgate
Livingston
Dalkeith
Airdrie
Whitburn
Gorebridge
Berwick-upon-Tweed
Motherwell
Wishaw
Penicuik
Lammermuir Hills
Duns
Carluke
Lauder
R. Tweed
Holy Island
Lanark
Peebles
Gala shiels
Coldstream
Farne Islands
Biggar
Melrose
Kelso
Tinto ▲707
Selkirk
Newtown St Boswells
Wooler
Broad Law ▲840
Ettrick Forest
R. Teviot
Jedburgh
The Cheviot ▲815
R. Breamish
Hart Fell ▲808
Ettrick Water
Hawick
Alnwick
Sanquhar
Moffat
R. Liddel
Kielder Water
Rothbury
Amble
Thornhill
R. Esk
Otterburn
R. Nith
Cheviot Hills
Morpeth
Ashington
Langholm
Lockerbie
Blyth
North R. Tyne
Cramlington
Ponteland
Whitley Bay
Dumfries
North Shields
R. Annan
Haltwhistle
Corbridge
Newcastle upon Tyne
South Shields
Gretna
R. Irthing
Hexham
Gateshead
Sunderland
Brampton
Derwent Reservoir
Stanley
Criffel ▲569
Annan
Carlisle
Consett
Chester-le-Street
Durham
Houghton le Spring
Dalbeattie
Wigton
Walsingham
Peterlee
Kirkcudbright
Maryport
Cross Fell ▲893
R. Wear
Spennymoor
Hartlepool
Cockermouth
Bassenthwaite Lake
Penrith
Cow Green Reservoir
Bishop Auckland
Tees Bay
Workington
Skiddaw ▲931
Keswick
R. Tees
Billingham
Redcar
Great Clifton
Derwent Water
Ullswater
Appleby-in-Westmorland
Barnard Castle
Newton Aycliffe
Darlington
Stockton-on-Tees
Middlesbrough
Hinderwell
Whitehaven
Shap
Kirkby Stephen
Richmond
Yarm
Thornaby-on-Tees
Guisborough
Whitby
St Bees Head
Helvellyn ▲949
Haweswater Reservoir
Catterick
Stokesley
Cleveland Hills
Lake District
Scafell Pike ▲977
Ambleside
High Seat ▲710
Round Hill ▲454
North York Moors
Seascale
Wast Water
Windermere
Sedbergh
Leeming
Northallerton
R. Rye
Burniston
Scarborough
Coniston
Kendal
Wensleydale
Helmsley
Pickering
Black Combe ▲600
Coniston Water
Leven
Hawes
R. Ure
Thirsk
Vale of Pickering
Filey
Milnthorpe
Kirkby Lonsdale
Whernside ▲736
R. Swale
Easingwold
Norton
Yorkshire Wolds
Millom
Ingleborough ▲724
Pen-y-Ghent ▲694
Great Whernside ▲703
Ripon
Flamborough
Barrow-in-Furness
Morecambe
Carnforth
Settle
Boroughbridge
Vale of York
Great Driffield
Bridlington
Isle of Walney
Morecambe Bay
Lancaster
Knaresborough
Haxby
Stamford Bridge
Hilpsford Point
Ward's Stone ▲560
Skipton
Harrogate
Wetherby
York
R. Ouse
Market Weighton
Beverley
Forest of Bowland
Penne Hill ▲557
Glusburn
Ilkley
Leven
Fleetwood
Clitheroe
Colne
Keighley
Bingley
Taddaster

Scale : One centimetre on this map is the same as 12.5 kilometres on the ground.

N O R T H   S E A

Key to symbols

- 🔵 Country capital
- ⦿ Main city/town
- ○ Other city/town
- ▬ Country boundary
- ▬ Road
- ▬ Railway
- ✈ Airport
- Lake
- River
- ▲ *Scafell Pike* Mountain and height in metres
  977

Land height above sea level in metres

- over 1500
- 1000 – 1500
- 900 – 1000
- 500 – 900
- 200 – 500
- 100 – 200
- 0 – 100

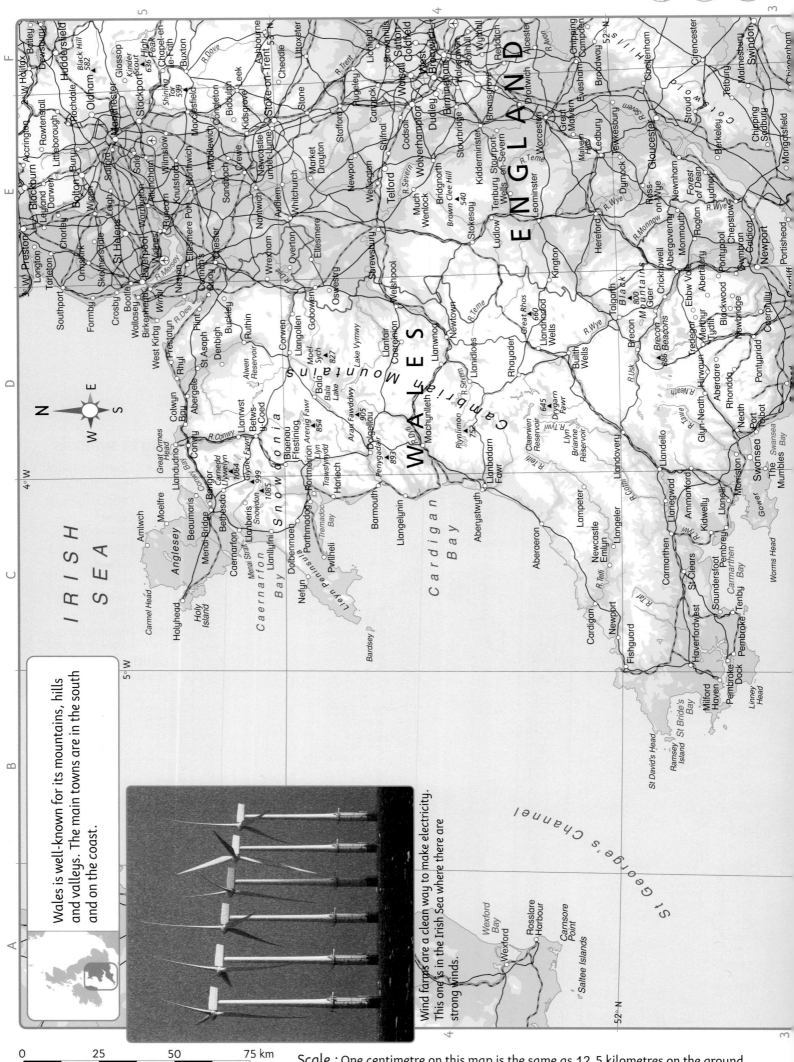

Wales is well-known for its mountains, hills and valleys. The main towns are in the south and on the coast.

Wind farms are a clean way to make electricity. This one is in the Irish Sea where there are strong winds.

Scale : One centimetre on this map is the same as 12.5 kilometres on the ground.

0   25   50   75 km

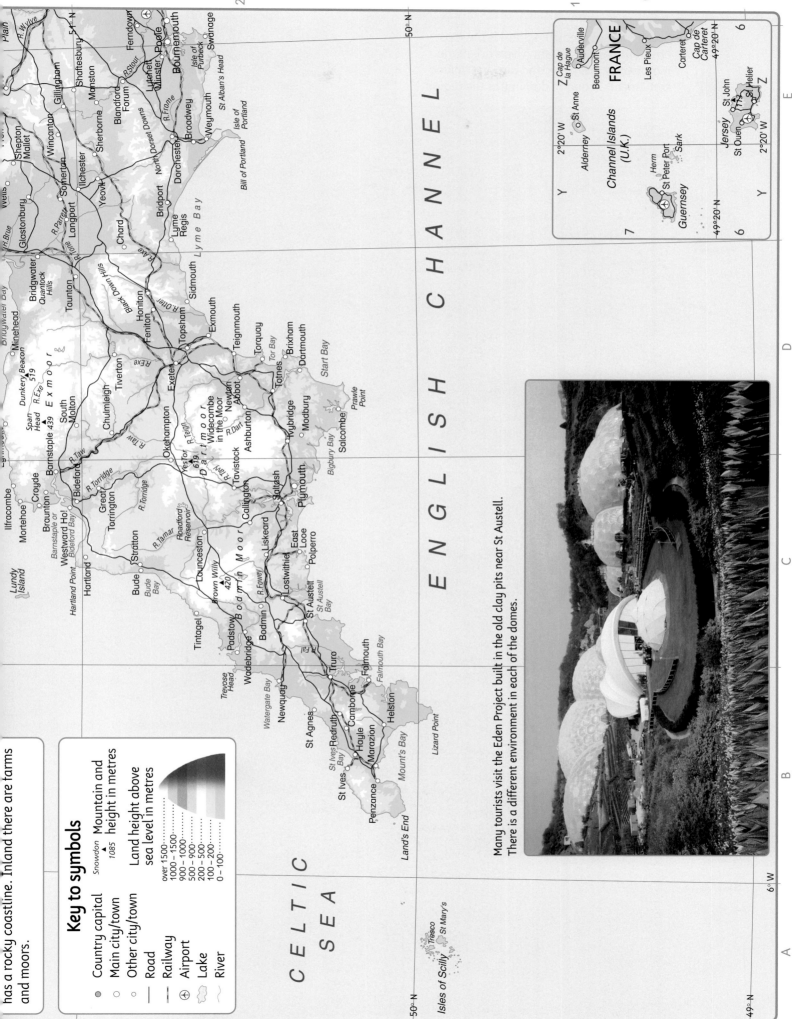

Many tourists visit the Eden Project built in the old clay pits near St Austell. There is a different environment in each of the domes.

Key to symbols

- Country capital
- Main city/town
- Other city/town
- Road
- Railway
- ✈ Airport
- Lake
- River

Snowdon Mountain and
▲
1085 height in metres

Land height above
sea level in metres

- over 1500
- 1000 – 1500
- 900 – 1000
- 500 – 900
- 200 – 500
- 100 – 200
- 0 – 100

has a rocky coastline. Inland there are farms and moors.

South and southeast England is the most crowded part of the UK. There are many motorways, railways and airports linking settlements. London dominates the region.

WALES

ENGLAND

Cambrian Mts

Penygadair 893

Machynlleth

Plynlimon 752

R. Dyfi

Llanfair Caereinion

Llanwnog

Newtown

Llanidloes

Rhayader

Claerwen Reservoir

Great Rhos 660

Drygarn Fawr 645

Llandrindod Wells

Llyn Brianne Reservoir

Builth Wells

Talgarth

R. Wye

R. Usk

Brecon

Black Mountains 800

Brecon Beacons 886

Crickhowell

Gaer

Abergavenny

Monmouth

Raglan

Glyn-Neath

Hirwaun

Tredegar

Merthyr Tydfil

Ebbw Vale

Abertillery

R. Neath

Neath

Aberdare

Blackwood

Newbridge

Pontypool

Cwmbran

Port Talbot

Rhondda

Pontypridd

Caerphilly

Porthcawl

Bridgend

Cowbridge

Clevedon

Penarth

Barry

Cardiff

Newport

Portishead

R. Monnow

Chepstow

Caldicot

Lydney

Forest of Dean

Newnham

Ross-on-Wye

R. Wye

Berkeley

Stroud

Shrewsbury

Welshpool

Wellington

Newport

Rugeley

Telford

Shifnal

Cannock

Codsall

Much Wenlock

Bridgnorth

Brown Clee Hill 540

Stokesay

Ludlow

Kidderminster

Stourport-on-Severn

Bromsgrove

Tenbury Wells

Leominster

R. Teme

Droitwich

Worcester

Great Malvern

Malvern Hills

Hereford

Ledbury

Dymock

Tewkesbury

R. Severn

Cheltenham

Gloucester

Burford

Witney

Cirencester

R. Thames

Tetbury

Malmesbury

Chipping Sodbury

Mangotsfield

Kingswood

Bristol

Bath

Melksham

Trowbridge

Radstock

Frome

Shepton Mallet

Glastonbury

Wells

Mendip Hills

Chew Valley Lake

Cheddar

Burnham-on-Sea

Bridgwater

Bridgwater Bay

Quantock Hills

Minehead

R. Exe

Dunkery Beacon 519

Exmoor

Lynmouth

Bristol Channel

Weston-super-Mare

Langport

Taunton

R. Tone

R. Parrett

Somerton

Ilchester

Wincanton

Gillingham

Shaftesbury

Sherborne

Yeovil

Chard

R. Brue

R. Axe

Tiverton

R. Exe

Black Down Hills

Feniton

Honiton

Chard

Lyme Regis

Bridport

North Dorset Downs

Dorchester

Broadway

Weymouth

Lyme Bay

Bill of Portland

Isle of Portland

St Alban's Head

Exeter

Topsham

Sidmouth

Exmouth

Newton Abbot

Ashburton

Teignmouth

Torquay

Tor Bay

Totnes

Brixham

Dartmouth

Start Bay

Prawle Point

Cannock

Lichfield

Brownhills

Tamworth

Walsall

Sutton Coldfield

Dudley

West Bromwich

Halesowen

Birmingham

Stourbridge

Solihull

Redditch

Alcester

Stratford-upon-Avon

Warwick

Coventry

Kenilworth

Royal Leamington Spa

Rugby

Daventry

Northampton

Chipping Campden

Banbury

Brackley

Buckingham

Milton Keynes

Bletchley

Stow-on-the-Wold

Chipping Norton

Bicester

Woodstock

Kidlington

Oxford

R. Cherwell

Leighton Buzzard

Dunstable

Aylesbury

R. Thame

Princes Risborough

Abingdon

Didcot

Stratton St Margaret

Swindon

Lambourn Downs

Chippenham

Marlborough

R. Kennet

Hungerford

Newbury

Kingsclere

Devizes

Burbage

Upavon

North Tidworth

Andover

Salisbury Plain

Warminster

R. Wylye

Salisbury

Winchester

New Alresford

Alton

Downton

Romsey

Eastleigh

Southampton

Hythe

Lyndhurst

New Forest

Brockenhurst

Lymington

Ringwood

Ferndown

Lytchett Minster

Poole

Wareham

Isle of Purbeck

Swanage

Christchurch

Bournemouth

Poole Bay

Yarmouth

Cowes

Newport

Isle of Wight

Shanklin

Ventnor

St. Catherine's Point

The Needles

The Solent

Ryde

Foreland

Gosport

Portsmouth

Fareham

Waterlooville

Havant

Chichester

Bognor Regis

Selsey

Littlehampton

Worthing

Reading

Twyford

Henley-on-Thames

Maidenhead

Marlow

Windsor

Bracknell

Wokingham

Staines

Slough

Uxbridge

LONDON

Sandhurst

Camberley

Woking

Farnborough

Aldershot

Fleet

Farnham

Basingstoke

Godalming

Guildford

Leatherhead

Dorking

Leith Hill 294

Cranleigh

Haslemere

Godalming

Reigate

Horley

Crawley

Billingshurst

Horsham

Petersfield

Midhurst

R. Rother

South Downs

Burgess Hill

Ripley

Belper

Ashbourne

Eastwood

Ilkeston

Cheadle

Uttoxeter

Derby

Nottingham

West Bridgford

Long Eaton

Castle Donnington

R. Trent

Burton upon Trent

Swadlincote

Shepshed

Kegworth

Loughborough

Coalville

Mountsorrel

Leicester

Oadby

Hinckley

Nuneaton

Lutterworth

Market Harborough

Wellingborough

Burton Latimer

Kettering

Rushden

R. Nene

Rounds

Huntingdon

Grafham Water

St Neots

Bedford

Olney

Newport Pagnell

Towcester

R. Tove

Bigg

Letchworth

Hitchin

Luton

Harpenden

St Albans

Hemel Hempstead

Chesham

Watford

High Wycombe

Ripley

Bingham

Newark-on-Trent

Long Bennington

Sleaford

Grantham

Colsterworth

Melton Mowbray

Oakham

Rutland Water

Uppingham

Corby

Oundle

Stamford

Market Deeping

Pinchbeck

Bourne

Sawtry

Peterborough

R. Welland

Newton Abbot

West Bridgford

Bletchley

Ashbourne

2° W   1° W   2° W   3° W   1° W

52° N   51° N   50° N

ENGLISH CHANNEL

A   B   C   D

Scale : One centimetre on this map is the same as 12.5 kilometres on the ground.

0   25   50   75 km

E · F · G · H

1° E   2° E   3° E   53° N

Key to symbols

- ■ Capital city
- ● Country capital
- ○ Main city/town
- ○ Other city/town
- — Country boundary
- — Road
- ╫ Railway
- ✈ Airport
- 〰 Lake
- 〰 River
- ▲ *Leith Hill* 294 Mountain and height in metres

Land height above sea level in metres

- over 1500
- 1000 – 1500
- 900 – 1000
- 500 – 900
- 200 – 500
- 100 – 200
- 0 – 100

Land below sea level

N O R T H S E A

The Wash

Hunstanton · Wells-next-the-Sea · Cromer

King's Lynn · Fakenham · Aylsham · North Walsham

Narborough · East Dereham · *R. Wensum* · Coltishall · Hoveton

Great R. Ouse · Swaffham · Norwich · *R. Bure*

Downham Market · Wymondham · *Norfolk Broads* · Great Yarmouth

Southery · Mundford · *R. Thet* · *R. Yare* · Corton

Littleport · Loddon · Lowestoft

Ely · Thetford · *Little R. Ouse* · Long Stratton · Bungay · Kessingland

Soham · Scole · *R. Waveney*

Stanton · *R. Dove* · Halesworth

market bridge · Bury St Edmunds · Saxmundham

N   D · Haverhill · Stowmarket · Wickham Market · Aldeburgh

Saffron Walden · Sudbury · Claydon · *Orford Ness*

Newport · Capel St Mary · Ipswich · 52° N

R. Colne · Halstead · *R. Stour* · Felixstowe

Braintree · Coggeshall · Colchester · Harwich

Bishop's Stortford · Great Dunmow · Brightlingsea · *The Naze* · Frinton-on-Sea

Witham · *R. Chelmer* · *R. Blackwater* · Clacton-on-Sea

Chelmsford · Maldon

Epping · Ingatestone · *R. Crouch* · Southminster

Ongar · Brentwood · Basildon · *Foulness Point*

South Ockendon · Rayleigh · Southend-on-Sea

Tilbury · *River Thames* · Grain · Sheerness

Gravesend · Isle of Sheppey · *Oosterschelde*

Rochester · Gillingham · Herne Bay · Margate · *North Foreland* · **NETHERLANDS**

Chatham · Whitstable · Isle of Thanet · Broadstairs · Goes

Sevenoaks · Sittingbourne · Faversham · Ramsgate · Vlissingen

Maidstone · Chilham · Canterbury · Eastry · *Westerschelde* · Terneuzen

North Downs · Barham · Deal · Zeebrugge

R. Medway · Ashford · Dover · Ostend · Brugge

Royal Tunbridge Wells · *R. Beult* · Sellindge · *Strait of Dover* · Nieuwpoort · **B E L G I U M** · Gent

the Weald · Hamstreet · Folkestone · Veurne

Crowborough · Hawkhurst · Hythe · *Channel Tunnel* · Dunkerque · Diksmuide · Tielt · *Schelde* · 54° N

Heathfield · Salehurst · *Romney Marsh* · New Romney · Calais · Gravelines · *Yser* · *Izer* · Roeselare · Oudenaarde

Hailsham · Rye · Lydd · Boulogne · *Ijzer* · Ieper · Kortrijk

Margate · Bexhill · Hastings · *Rye Bay* · *Dungeness* · Guînes · **F R A N C E** · Mouscron · Ronse

Eastbourne · Wimereux · St-Omer · 164 ▲ *Mont des Cats* · Roubaix

Beachy Head · Boulogne · Hazebrouck

London, one of the world's largest cities, grew up as a port at the lowest crossing on the River Thames.

E

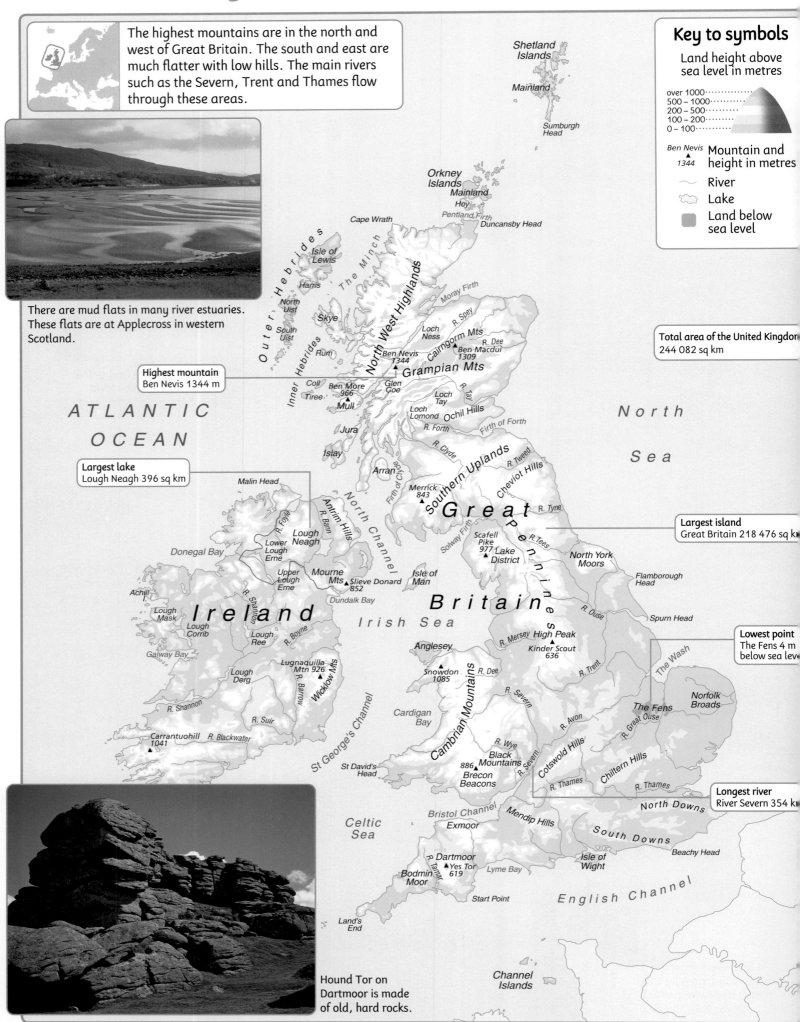

The highest mountains are in the north and west of Great Britain. The south and east are much flatter with low hills. The main rivers such as the Severn, Trent and Thames flow through these areas.

Key to symbols

Land height above sea level in metres

over 1000 ·················
500 – 1000 ·················
200 – 500 ·················
100 – 200 ·················
0 – 100 ·················

Ben Nevis
▲ Mountain and height in metres
1344

— River

Lake

Land below sea level

There are mud flats in many river estuaries. These flats are at Applecross in western Scotland.

Highest mountain
Ben Nevis 1344 m

Largest lake
Lough Neagh 396 sq km

Total area of the United Kingdom
244 082 sq km

Largest island
Great Britain 218 476 sq km

Lowest point
The Fens 4 m below sea level

Longest river
River Severn 354 km

ATLANTIC OCEAN

North Sea

Irish Sea

Ireland

Great Britain

Celtic Sea

English Channel

Shetland Islands
Mainland
Sumburgh Head

Orkney Islands
Mainland
Hoy
Pentland Firth
Duncansby Head

Cape Wrath

Outer Hebrides
Isle of Lewis
Harris
North Uist
South Uist
Skye
Rum
The Minch

North West Highlands
Loch Ness
R. Spey
Cairngorm Mts
R. Dee
Ben Macdui 1309
Ben Nevis 1344
Grampian Mts
Glen Coe
Moray Firth

Coll
Tiree
Ben More 966
Mull
Inner Hebrides

Jura

Islay

Arran

Firth of Clyde

Loch Tay
R. Tay
Loch Lomond
Ochil Hills
R. Forth
Firth of Forth
R. Clyde

Southern Uplands
R. Tweed
Cheviot Hills

Merrick 843

Malin Head
Donegal Bay
Achill
Lough Mask
Lough Corrib
Galway Bay
Lough Derg
R. Shannon
R. Suir
Carrantuohill 1041
R. Blackwater
Lugnaquilla Mtn 926
Wicklow Mts
R. Barrow
R. Boyne
Lough Ree
R. Shannon

R. Foyle
Lower Lough Erne
Upper Lough Erne
Lough Neagh
R. Bann
Antrim Hills
North Channel

Mourne Mts
Slieve Donard 852
Dundalk Bay

Isle of Man

Solway Firth
Scafell Pike 977
Lake District

Pennines

North York Moors
R. Tees
R. Tyne
R. Ouse
Flamborough Head
Spurn Head

High Peak
Kinder Scout 636
R. Mersey

Anglesey
Snowdon 1085
R. Dee
Cambrian Mountains
Cardigan Bay

Black Mountains 886
Brecon Beacons
R. Wye
R. Severn
R. Trent
R. Avon
R. Severn

The Wash
R. Great Ouse
The Fens
Norfolk Broads

Cotswold Hills
Chiltern Hills
R. Thames
R. Thames

St George's Channel
St David's Head

Bristol Channel
Exmoor
Mendip Hills
North Downs
South Downs
Beachy Head
Isle of Wight

Dartmoor
Yes Tor 619
R. Tamar
Bodmin Moor
Lyme Bay
Start Point

Land's End

Channel Islands

Hound Tor on Dartmoor is made of old, hard rocks.

0   50   100   150   200   250 km

Scale : One centimetre on this map is the same as 50 kilometres on the ground.

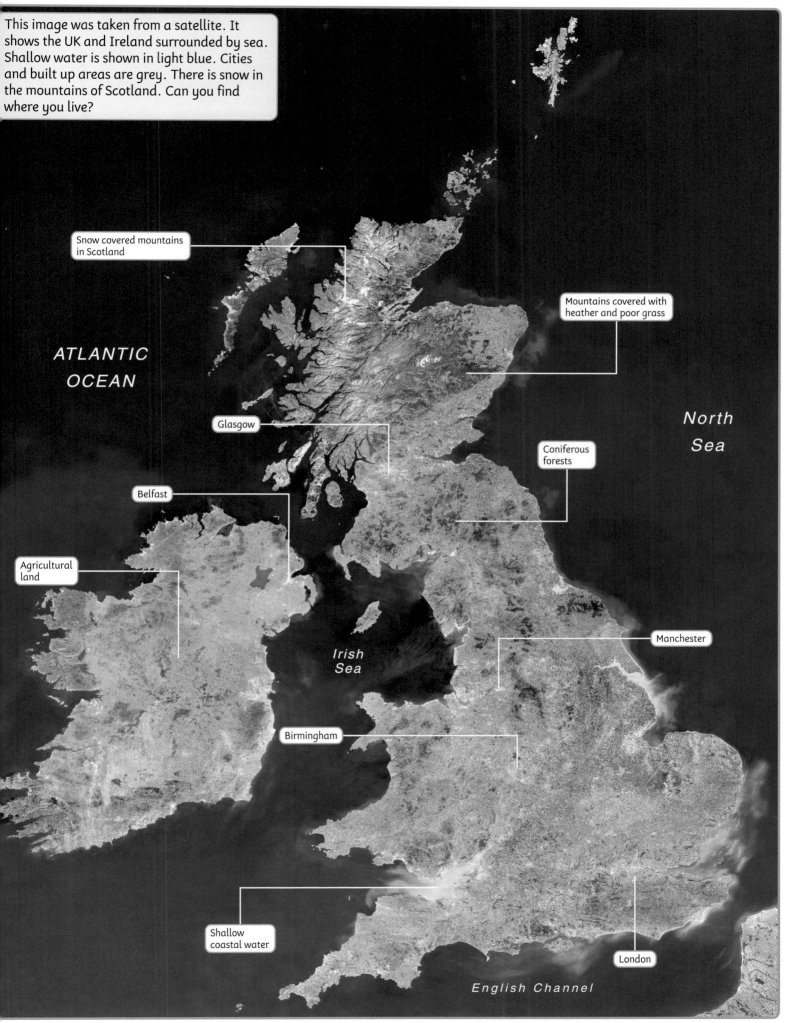

This image was taken from a satellite. It shows the UK and Ireland surrounded by sea. Shallow water is shown in light blue. Cities and built up areas are grey. There is snow in the mountains of Scotland. Can you find where you live?

Snow covered mountains in Scotland

Mountains covered with heather and poor grass

ATLANTIC OCEAN

North Sea

Glasgow

Coniferous forests

Belfast

Agricultural land

Manchester

Irish Sea

Birmingham

Shallow coastal water

London

English Channel

The mixture of sun, rain and wind make the weather.

Extreme weather causes problems. In July 2007 torrential rain flooded Tewkesbury and other parts of central England.

Annual rainfall

All parts of the UK have rain throughout the year. Western areas are the wettest. Here winds from the sea shed water as they rise over the mountains.

Average annual rainfall
- more than 2000 mm
- 1500 – 2000 mm
- 1000 – 1500 mm
- 750 – 1000 mm
- 625 – 750 mm
- less than 625 mm
- Location of places on climate graphs

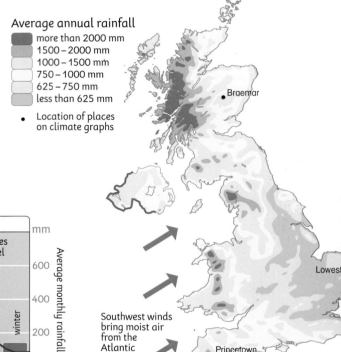

Southwest winds bring moist air from the Atlantic Ocean

Seasonal climate graphs

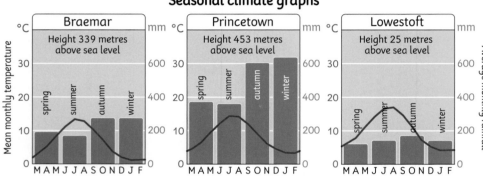

Winter temperatures

In January, warm ocean currents bring milder conditions to the southwest of the UK. The coldest areas are the mountains in the north.

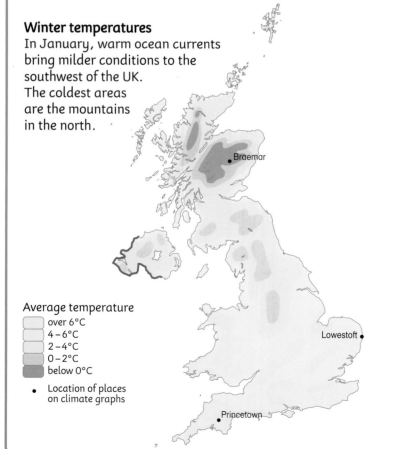

Average temperature
- over 6°C
- 4 – 6°C
- 2 – 4°C
- 0 – 2°C
- below 0°C
- Location of places on climate graphs

Summer temperatures

In July, the warmest parts of the UK are in the south, especially along the coasts. Mountain areas are the coolest.

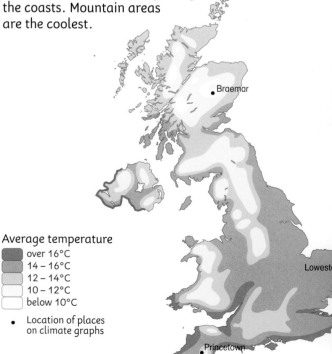

Average temperature
- over 16°C
- 14 – 16°C
- 12 – 14°C
- 10 – 12°C
- below 10°C
- Location of places on climate graphs

Country populations

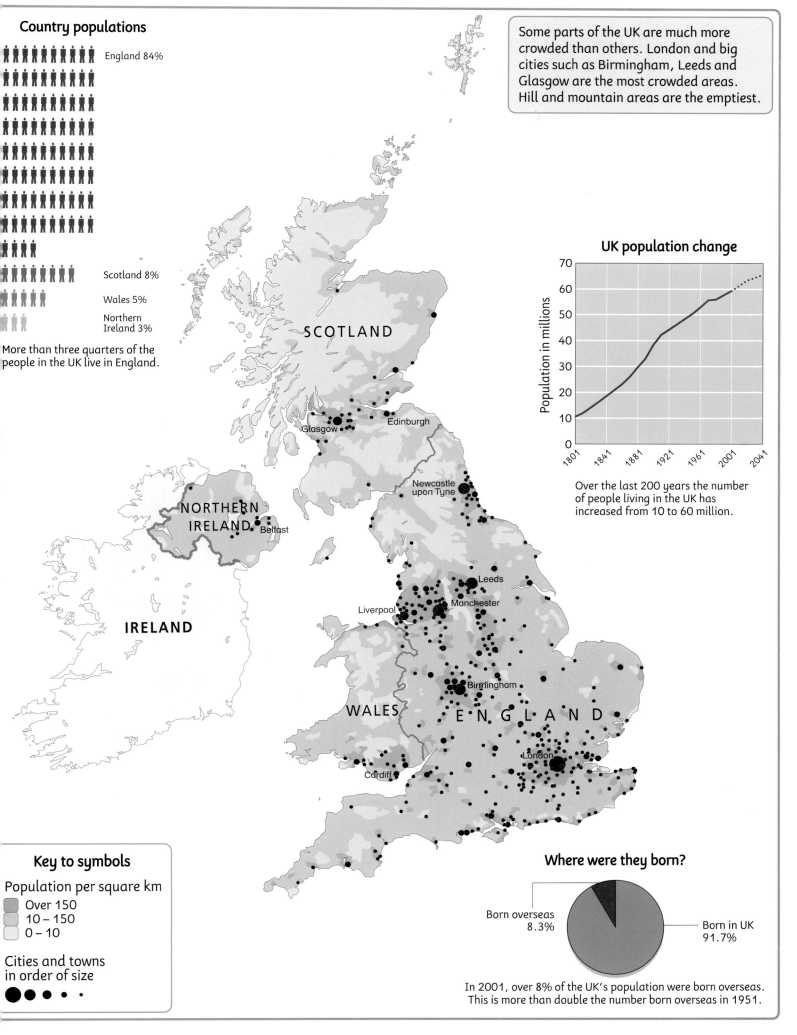

England 84%

Scotland 8%

Wales 5%

Northern Ireland 3%

More than three quarters of the people in the UK live in England.

Some parts of the UK are much more crowded than others. London and big cities such as Birmingham, Leeds and Glasgow are the most crowded areas. Hill and mountain areas are the emptiest.

SCOTLAND

Glasgow   Edinburgh

NORTHERN IRELAND   Belfast

IRELAND

Newcastle upon Tyne

Leeds

Liverpool   Manchester

Birmingham

WALES   E N G L A N D

Cardiff   London

UK population change

Over the last 200 years the number of people living in the UK has increased from 10 to 60 million.

Key to symbols

Population per square km

- Over 150
- 10 – 150
- 0 – 10

Cities and towns in order of size

Where were they born?

Born overseas 8.3%

Born in UK 91.7%

In 2001, over 8% of the UK's population were born overseas. This is more than double the number born overseas in 1951.

50   100   150   200   250 km

Scale : One centimetre on this map is the same as 50 kilometres on the ground.

Roads and railways link the main cities in the UK. There are ferry services to mainland Europe, Ireland and other islands. Some places also have airports. How many can you find on the map?

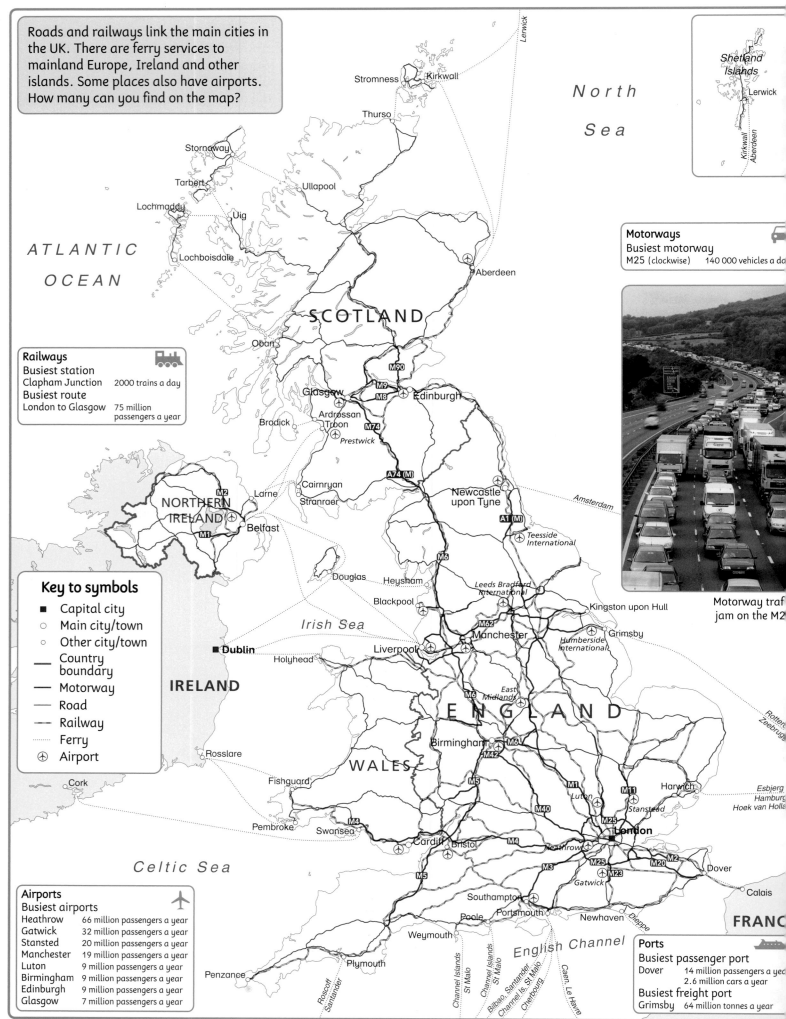

Railways
Busiest station
Clapham Junction   2000 trains a day
Busiest route
London to Glasgow   75 million passengers a year

Motorways
Busiest motorway
M25 (clockwise)   140 000 vehicles a day

Motorway traffic jam on the M2

Key to symbols
- ■ Capital city
- ○ Main city/town
- ○ Other city/town
- — Country boundary
- ▬ Motorway
- — Road
- ╫ Railway
- ⋯ Ferry
- ⊕ Airport

Airports
Busiest airports
Heathrow   66 million passengers a year
Gatwick   32 million passengers a year
Stansted   20 million passengers a year
Manchester 19 million passengers a year
Luton   9 million passengers a year
Birmingham 9 million passengers a year
Edinburgh   9 million passengers a year
Glasgow   7 million passengers a year

Ports
Busiest passenger port
Dover   14 million passengers a year
         2.6 million cars a year
Busiest freight port
Grimsby   64 million tonnes a year

North Sea

Shetland Islands
Lerwick

ATLANTIC OCEAN

Irish Sea

Celtic Sea

English Channel

IRELAND

NORTHERN IRELAND

SCOTLAND

ENGLAND

WALES

FRANCE

Stornoway, Tarbert, Lochmaddy, Uig, Ullapool, Lochboisdale, Stromness, Kirkwall, Thurso, Aberdeen, Oban, Glasgow, Ardrossan, Troon, Prestwick, Brodick, Edinburgh, Newcastle upon Tyne, Teesside International, Larne, Stranraer, Cairnryan, Belfast, Dublin, Douglas, Heysham, Blackpool, Leeds Bradford International, Kingston upon Hull, Grimsby, Humberside International, Liverpool, Manchester, Holyhead, East Midlands, Birmingham, Fishguard, Rosslare, Cork, Pembroke, Swansea, Cardiff, Bristol, London, Heathrow, Gatwick, Stansted, Luton, Harwich, Southampton, Portsmouth, Poole, Weymouth, Plymouth, Penzance, Newhaven, Dover, Calais

M90, M9, M8, M74, A74(M), M6, M62, M1, A1(M), M5, M6, M42, M40, M4, M3, M25, M23, M20, M2, M11, M1, M2

0 40 80 120 160 200 km

Scale : One centimetre on this map is the same as 40 kilometres on the ground.

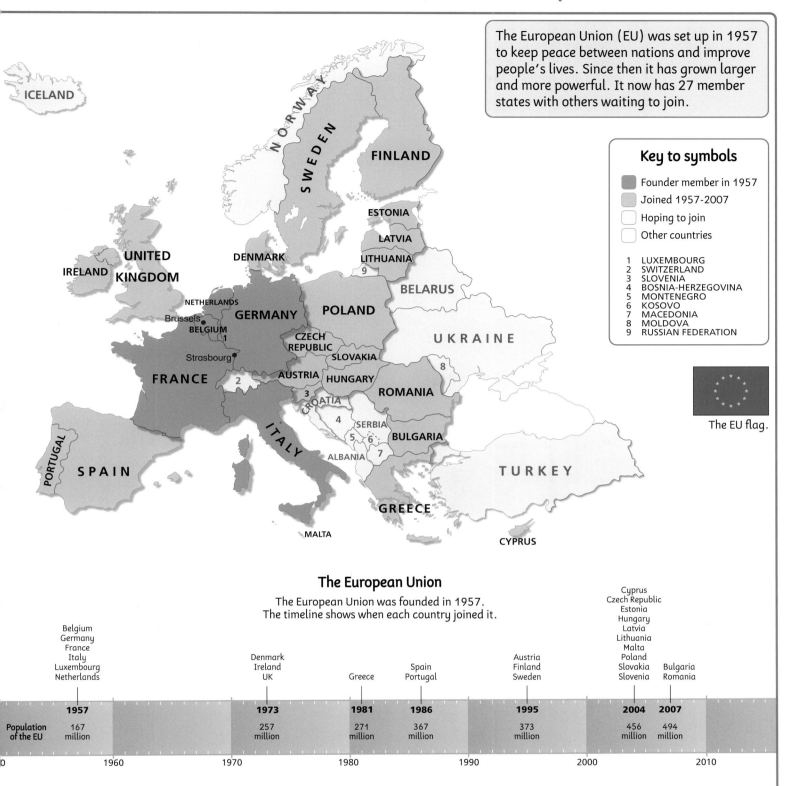

The European Union (EU) was set up in 1957 to keep peace between nations and improve people's lives. Since then it has grown larger and more powerful. It now has 27 member states with others waiting to join.

ICELAND

NORWAY
SWEDEN
FINLAND
ESTONIA
LATVIA
LITHUANIA
DENMARK
UNITED KINGDOM
IRELAND
NETHERLANDS
BELARUS
GERMANY
POLAND
Brussels
BELGIUM
1
CZECH REPUBLIC
UKRAINE
SLOVAKIA
Strasbourg
FRANCE
2
AUSTRIA
HUNGARY
8
3
ROMANIA
CROATIA
4
SERBIA
5 6
BULGARIA
ALBANIA 7
PORTUGAL
ITALY
SPAIN
TURKEY
GREECE
MALTA
CYPRUS

Key to symbols

■	Founder member in 1957
■	Joined 1957-2007
□	Hoping to join
□	Other countries

1 LUXEMBOURG
2 SWITZERLAND
3 SLOVENIA
4 BOSNIA-HERZEGOVINA
5 MONTENEGRO
6 KOSOVO
7 MACEDONIA
8 MOLDOVA
9 RUSSIAN FEDERATION

The EU flag.

The European Union

The European Union was founded in 1957.
The timeline shows when each country joined it.

	1957	1973	1981	1986	1995	2004	2007
	Belgium Germany France Italy Luxembourg Netherlands	Denmark Ireland UK	Greece	Spain Portugal	Austria Finland Sweden	Cyprus Czech Republic Estonia Hungary Latvia Lithuania Malta Poland Slovakia Slovenia	Bulgaria Romania
Population of the EU	167 million	257 million	271 million	367 million	373 million	456 million	494 million

1960   1970   1980   1990   2000   2010

European laws are made in the parliament which meets in Brussels and Strasbourg. This photograph shows the Government Building of the European Union in Strasbourg.

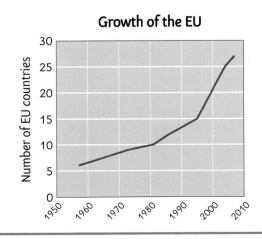

Growth of the EU

Number of EU countries

30
25
20
15
10
5
0

1950 1960 1970 1980 1990 2000 2010

There are over 40 countries in Europe.
Ukraine and France are the largest.
Malta and Andorra are two of the smallest.

ARCTIC OCEAN

Novaya Zemlya

Total population of Europe
(excluding Russian Federation)
591 million

Russian Federation
Area 17 million sq km
Population 141 milli...

ICELAND
■ Reykjavík

ATLANTIC OCEAN

Jan Mayen (Norway)

Country with most people
(excluding Russian Federation)
Germany 82 million

R U S S I A N

F E D E R A T I O N

White Sea

Faroe Islands (Denmark)

N O R W A Y

S W E D E N

F I N L A N D

Gulf of Bothnia

■ Oslo
■ Stockholm
Helsinki ■
○ St Petersburg

Tallinn ■
ESTONIA
LATVIA
Rīga ■
○ Moscow

○ Edinburgh *North Sea*
Belfast ○
UNITED KINGDOM
Dublin ○
IRELAND

DENMARK
Copenhagen ■

Baltic Sea

LITHUANIA
Vilnius ■
Minsk ■

BELARUS

Largest country
(excluding Russian Federation)
Ukraine 603 700 sq km

■ London

English Channel

Berlin ■
GERMANY

Warsaw ■
POLAND

Kiev ■

U K R A I N E

○ Volgograd

1
2
3
Prague ■
CZECH REPUBLIC

■ **Paris**

Largest city
(Western Europe)
Paris 10 million

FRANCE

Munich ○

Bay of Biscay

Lyon ○

4

Vienna ■
Bratislava ■
AUSTRIA
HUNGARY
Budapest ■

SLOVAKIA

MOLDOVA
Chişinău ■
Odesa ○

5
Zagreb ■
Belgrade ■
SERBIA
ROMANIA
Bucharest ■

Caspian Sea

Milan ○

SAN MARINO

6
7 8
9
Sofia ■
BULGARIA

Skopje ■

Black Sea

Largest city
Istanbul 11 million

Corsica

Rome ■
ITALY

Adriatic Sea

Tirana ■
ALBANIA

○ Istanbul
TURKEY

PORTUGAL
ANDORRA

Lisbon ■
Madrid ■
SPAIN
○ Barcelona

Balearic Islands
Palma de Mallorca ○

Sardinia

GREECE

Aegean Sea

A S I A

Strait of Gibraltar
Gibraltar (UK) ○

Sicily

■ Athens

Mediterranean Sea

Crete

Rhodes

MALTA

A F R I C A

1 NETHERLANDS
2 BELGIUM
3 LUXEMBOURG
4 SWITZERLAND
5 SLOVENIA
6 BOSNIA-HERZEGOVINA
7 MONTENEGRO
8 KOSOVO
9 MACEDONIA
10 RUSSIAN FEDERATION

Key to symbols

◢ Countries
■ Capital city
○ Important city/town

Ancient buildings around
Red Square, Moscow.

0 250 500 750 1000 1250 1500 km

Scale : One centimetre on this map is the same as 250 kilometres on the ground.

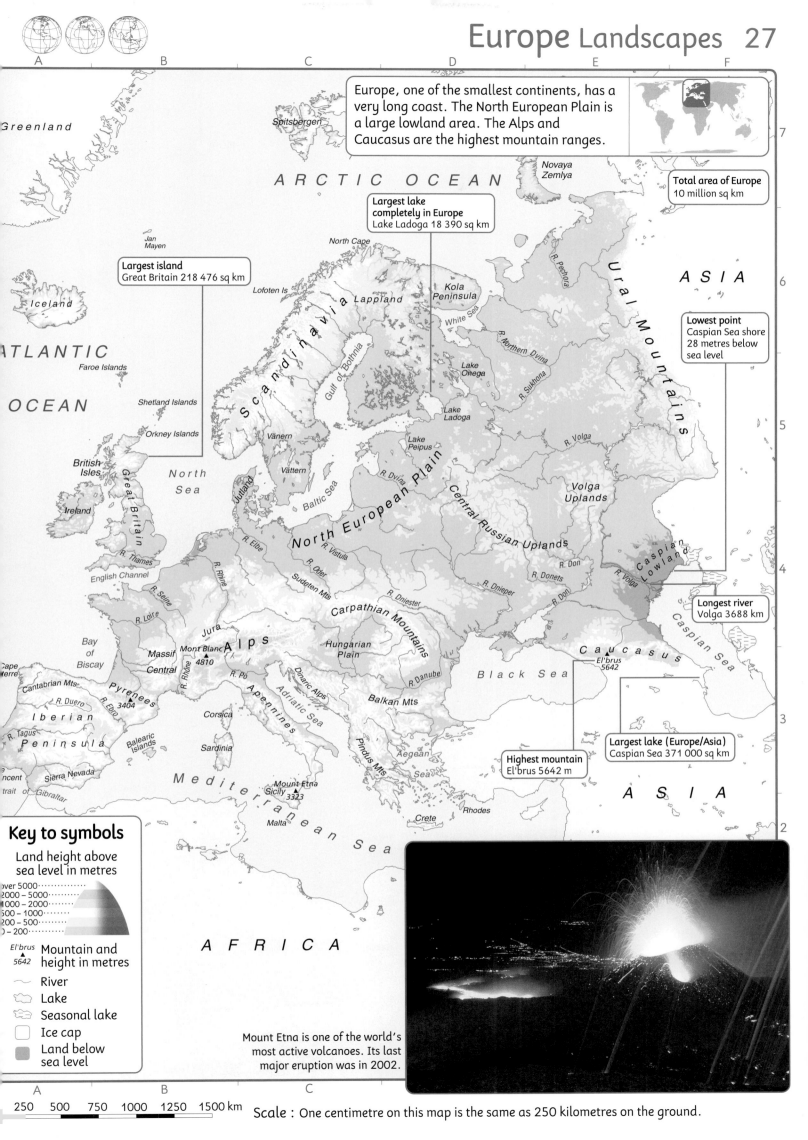

Europe, one of the smallest continents, has a very long coast. The North European Plain is a large lowland area. The Alps and Caucasus are the highest mountain ranges.

Total area of Europe
10 million sq km

Largest lake completely in Europe
Lake Ladoga 18 390 sq km

Largest island
Great Britain 218 476 sq km

Lowest point
Caspian Sea shore 28 metres below sea level

Longest river
Volga 3688 km

Largest lake (Europe/Asia)
Caspian Sea 371 000 sq km

Highest mountain
El'brus 5642 m

ARCTIC OCEAN

ASIA

AFRICA

Greenland
Spitsbergen
Novaya Zemlya
Ural Mountains
Iceland
Jan Mayen
North Cape
Kola Peninsula
White Sea
R. Pechora
ATLANTIC OCEAN
Faroe Islands
Lofoten Is
Scandinavia
Lappland
R. Northern Dvina
Lake Onega
R. Sukhona
Shetland Islands
Orkney Islands
Vänern
Gulf of Bothnia
Lake Ladoga
R. Volga
British Isles
North Sea
Vättern
Lake Peipus
Volga Uplands
Great Britain
Ireland
Jutland
Baltic Sea
R. Dvina
North European Plain
Central Russian Uplands
R. Thames
R. Elbe
R. Vistula
R. Don
R. Donets
Caspian Lowland
English Channel
R. Seine
R. Rhine
R. Oder
Sudeten Mts
R. Dniester
R. Dnieper
R. Don
R. Volga
Caspian Sea
R. Loire
Carpathian Mountains
Bay of Biscay
Massif Central
Mont Blanc 4810
Alps
Jura
R. Rhône
Hungarian Plain
R. Danube
Caucasus
El'brus 5642
Cape Ferre
Cantabrian Mts
R. Duero
Pyrenees 3404
R. Ebro
R. Po
Apennines
Dinaric Alps
Adriatic Sea
Balkan Mts
Black Sea
Iberian Peninsula
R. Tagus
Corsica
Sierra Nevada
Balearic Islands
Sardinia
Pindus Mts
Aegean Sea
Strait of Gibraltar
Mediterranean Sea
Mount Etna Sicily 3323
Malta
Crete
Rhodes
ASIA

Key to symbols

Land height above sea level in metres

over 5000
2000 – 5000
1000 – 2000
500 – 1000
200 – 500
0 – 200

El'brus ▲ 5642 Mountain and height in metres

∿ River

Lake

Seasonal lake

Ice cap

Land below sea level

Mount Etna is one of the world's most active volcanoes. Its last major eruption was in 2002.

Scale : One centimetre on this map is the same as 250 kilometres on the ground.

250 500 750 1000 1250 1500 km

Three Scandinavian countries – Norway, Sweden and Denmark – lie at the heart of northern Europe. They have similar traditions and beliefs. In the past, the people who lived there also all spoke the same language.

N
W E
S

ICELAND
Akureyri
Arctic Circle
Reykjavík
Vatnajökull
Seyðisfjörður

Lofoten Islands
Tromsø
Narvik
Bodø
NORWAY

Norwegian Sea

Trondheim
Östersund
Ålesund
Sundsva
Galdhøpiggen 2470
Lillehammer
Bergen
SWEDEN

Faroe Islands (Denmark)

Uppsalo
Oslo
Drammen
Västerås
Stoc
Karlstad
Stavanger
Örebro
Vänern
Kristiansand
Norrköping
Shetland Islands
Gothenburg
Vättern
Gotlan
Skagerrak
Jönköping

ATLANTIC OCEAN

60° N

Outer Hebrides
Orkney Islands
North Sea
Aalborg
Öland
Inverness
Ben Nevis 1344
Grampian Mountains
Aberdeen
DENMARK
Halmstad
Karlskrona
Glasgow
Dundee
Århus
55° N
Kattegat

Londonderry
Edinburgh
UNITED KINGDOM
Esbjerg
Copenhagen
Odense
Belfast
Carlisle
Newcastle upon Tyne
Malmö
Bornholm
Galway
IRELAND
Irish Sea
KINGDOM
Kiel
Limerick
Blackpool
Leeds
Rostock
Gdańsk
Dublin
Liverpool
Manchester
Koszalin
Cork
Sheffield
Groningen
Hamburg
Szczecin
Wexford
Birmingham
Nottingham
NETHERLANDS
Bremen
Bydgoszcz
Norwich
Amsterdam
IJsselmeer
Hannover
R. Elbe
Swansea
Oxford
The Hague
Poznań
Cardiff
R. Thames
London
Rotterdam
Duisburg
Bielefeld
Magdeburg
Berlin
POL
Bristol
Dortmund
R. Weser
Essen
GERMANY
R. Oder
Plymouth
Southampton
Dover
Brugge
Eindhoven
Düsseldorf
Zielona Góra
Wroclaw
Strait of Dover
Calais
Antwerp
Cologne
Leipzig
English Channel
Lille
BELGIUM
Brussels
Bonn
Dresden
Sudeten Mts.
Channel Islands
Le Havre
Amiens
Liège
Erfurt
Ostra
Brest
Rouen
LUXEMBOURG
Frankfurt
Prague
Rennes
Caen
Luxembourg
Mainz
Nuremberg
CZECH REPUBLIC
Reims
Nancy
Karlsruhe
Plzeň
Brno
Paris
R. Seine
Stuttgart
R. Danube
Le Mans
Strasbourg
Vienna
Brati
Nantes
Orléans
R. Loire
R. Seine
Munich
R. Inn
Linz
Buda
La Rochelle
Tours
Basel
Zürich
Salzburg
H
Poitiers
FRANCE
Dijon
Bern
SWITZERLAND
Innsbruck
LIECHTENSTEIN
AUSTRIA
Graz

0°
5° E
10° E
15° E
20° E

50° N
45° N
5° W

Scale : One centimetre on this map is the same as 100 kilometres on the grou

0 100 200 300 400 500 600 700 800 km

L M N O P Q R

30° E   35° E   40° E   45° E   50° E   55° E

Arctic Circle

Barents Sea

Kirkenes
Murmansk

Kola Peninsula

Kandalaksha

Mezen'
R. Mezen'
Ukhta

65° N

6

White Sea

Archangel
Severodvinsk
Belomorsk

R. Northern Dvina

Kotlas

5

Sukyvkar

Oulu

F I N L A N D

Kuopio

Medvezh'yegorsk

Petrozavodsk
Lake Onega

Konosha

R. Sukhona

60° N

4

Tampere
Lahti

Lake Ladoga

St Petersburg

Cherepovets   Vologda

Kostroma

juväskylä

Vantaa
● Helsinki

Gulf of Finland

Rybinsk Reservoir
Rybinsk
R. Volga
Yaroslavl'
Ivanovo

Nizhniy Novgorod

Vladimir

55° N

3

● Tallinn

E S T O N I A
Pärnu   Tartu

Lake Peipus

Velikiy Novgorod

R U S S I A N

Tver'

Gulf of Riga

L A T V I A
● Riga
R. Dvina

Pskov

Velikiye Luki

Moscow ■

F E D E R A T I O N

Ryazan'

Saransk

juliai
Daugavpils

Vitsyebsk

Kaluga
Tula

Tambov

T H U A N I A

Orsha
Smolensk

D.   Kaunas
● Vilnius

Bryansk

Orel

Lipetsk

Balashov

Mahilyow

Minsk ■

B E L A R U S
Babruysk
R. Dniepr

Kursk
Voronezh'
Borisoglebsk

Hrodna
Baranavichy

Homyel'

Belgorod

50° N

yrstok
Mazyr
Chernihiv
Sumy

R. Don

rsaw
Brest

Kiev ■

U K R A I N E

ublin
Rivne
Zhytomyr

L'vov
Khmel'nyts'kyy
Vinnytsya

R. Dniester

Carpathian Mountains
Chernivtsi

Bălti

šice
Pietrosa 2305

MOLDOVA ● Chişinău

Satu Mare

skola
R O M A N I A

Cluj-Napoca   Bacău

25° E

K L M N

Key to symbols

■ Capital city
○ Main city/town
○ Other city/town
— Country boundary
— Road
—— Railway
⌇ Canal
⊕ Airport
🏞 Lake
〜 River

☐ Ice cap
Galdhøpiggen ▲ Mountain and height in metres
2470

Land height above sea level in metres
over 5000
3000 – 5000
2000 – 3000
1000 – 2000
500 – 1000
200 – 500
0 – 200

▨ Land below sea level

Iceland is famous for hot springs and geysers. As well as attracting tourists, geysers are a valuable source of power.

Capital populations

Millions

London   Paris   Brussels   Oslo   Berlin   Prague   Moscow

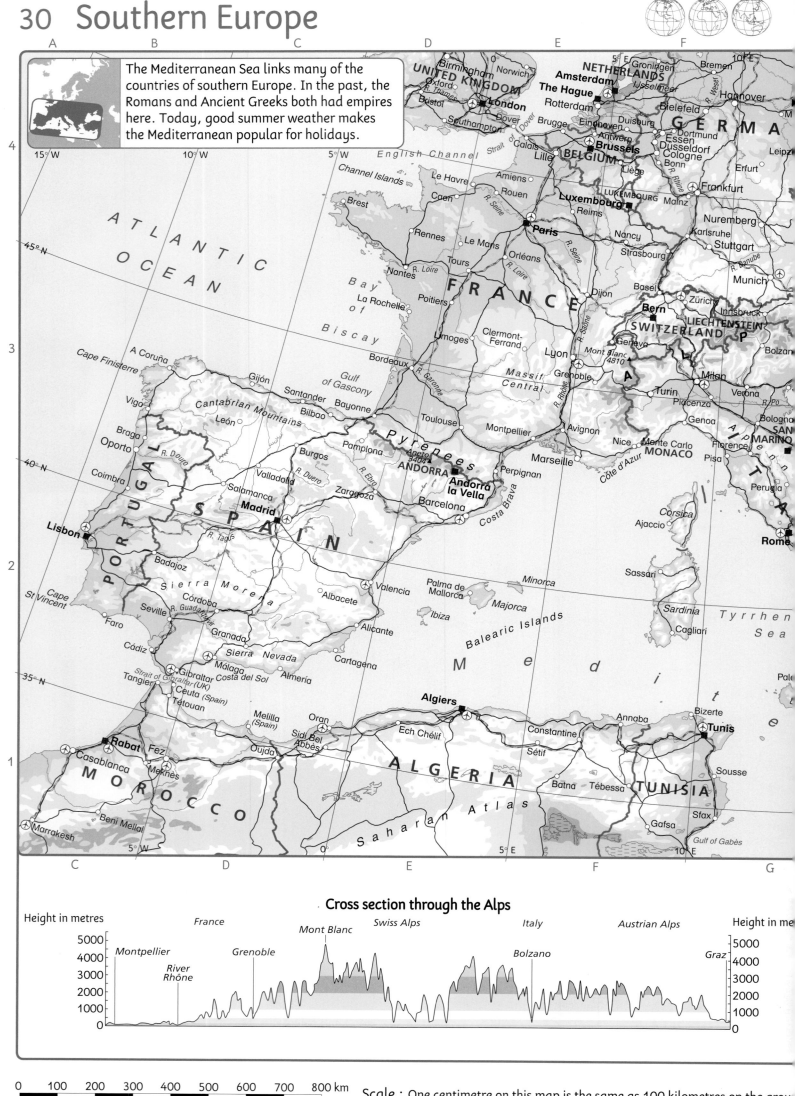

The Mediterranean Sea links many of the countries of southern Europe. In the past, the Romans and Ancient Greeks both had empires here. Today, good summer weather makes the Mediterranean popular for holidays.

ATLANTIC OCEAN

UNITED KINGDOM
Birmingham
Norwich
Oxford
R. Thames
Bristol
London
Southampton
Dover
Strait of Dover
Calais
Lille
Brussels
BELGIUM
Amiens
Rouen
Reims
Paris
Le Havre
Caen
Brest
Channel Islands
English Channel

NETHERLANDS
Amsterdam
The Hague
Rotterdam
Antwerp
Eindhoven
Duisburg
Düsseldorf
Cologne
Bonn
Liège
Luxembourg
LUXEMBOURG
Mainz
Nancy
Strasbourg
Groningen
IJsselmeer
Bielefeld
GERMA
Dortmund
Essen
Erfurt
Frankfurt
Nuremberg
Karlsruhe
Stuttgart
Bremen
Hannover
R. Weser

Rennes
Le Mans
Nantes
R. Loire
Tours
Poitiers
La Rochelle
Bay of Biscay
Gulf of Gascony

FRANCE
Orléans
R. Seine
R. Loire
Dijon
Limoges
Clermont-Ferrand
Massif Central
Lyon
Grenoble
R. Rhône
R. Saône
Basel
Bern
SWITZERLAND
Geneva
Mont Blanc 4810
Munich
Zürich
Innsbruck
LIECHTENSTEIN
Bolzano
Turin
Milan
Verona
R. Po
P
A

Montpellier
Avignon
Marseille
Nice
Monte Carlo
MONACO
Côte d'Azur
Genoa
Florence
Pisa
Perugia
SAN MARINO
Bologna
Rome
A
Corsica
Ajaccio
Sardinia
Cagliari
Sassari
Tyrrhen Sea

A Coruña
Cape Finisterre
Vigo
Braga
Oporto
Coimbra
Lisbon
Cape St Vincent
PORTUGAL
R. Douro
Gijón
Santander
Bilbao
León
Cantabrian Mountains
Burgos
Valladolid
Salamanca
Madrid
R. Duero
R. Tagus
Badajoz
Sierra Morena
Córdoba
R. Guadalquivir
Seville
Faro
Cádiz
SPAIN
Bayonne
Pamplona
Zaragoza
R. Ebro
Toulouse
Pyrenees
Aneto 3404
ANDORRA
Andorra la Vella
Barcelona
Costa Brava
Perpignan
Valencia
Palma de Mallorca
Minorca
Majorca
Ibiza
Balearic Islands
Albacete
Alicante
Cartagena
Granada
Sierra Nevada
Málaga
Almería
Costa del Sol
Gibraltar (UK)
Ceuta (Spain)
Strait of Gibraltar
Tangier
Tétouan
Melilla (Spain)
Oran
Sidi Bel Abbès
Oujda

Rabat
Casablanca
Meknès
Fez
Marrakesh
Beni Mellal
MOROCCO
Ech Chélif
Algiers
ALGERIA
Saharan Atlas
Constantine
Sétif
Batna
Tébessa
Annaba
Bizerte
Tunis
TUNISIA
Sousse
Sfax
Gafsa
Gulf of Gabès

Mediterranean

Cross section through the Alps

Height in metres
France
Mont Blanc
Swiss Alps
Italy
Austrian Alps
Height in me
Montpellier
River Rhône
Grenoble
Bolzano
Graz
5000
4000
3000
2000
1000
0

Scale : One centimetre on this map is the same as 100 kilometres on the grou

0 100 200 300 400 500 600 700 800 km

H   I   J   K   L   M

20° E   25° E   30° E   35° E   40° E   50° N

Bydgoszcz   R. Vistula   Białystok   Baranavichy   Mazyr   Homyel'   Chernihiv   Kursk   Belgorod

BELARUS

Poznań   **Warsaw**   Brest   Sumy

POLAND

lona   Łódź   Lublin   **Kiev**   Khar'kov   Morozovsk

Wrocław   R. Oder   R. Vistula   Rivne   Zhytomyr   R. Donets   Luhans'k   **RUSSIAN**

Sudeten Mts   Katowice   R. Vistula   L'vov   Khmel'nyts'kyy   Vinnytsya   Horlivka   Donets'k   Rostov-na-Donu   **FEDERATION**

Ostrava   Kraków   **UKRAINE**   Kirovograd   Dnipropetrovs'k   Zaporizhzhya   Tikhoretsk

CZECH   Brno   **SLOVAKIA**   Košice   R. Dniester   Chernivtsi   Kryvyy Rih   Mariupol'

REPUBLIC   Carpathian Mountains   Melitopol'

enna   **Bratislava**   Miskolc   R. Tisza   Debrecen   Satu Mare   Pietrosa 2305   Bălţi   **MOLDOVA**   Mykolayiv   R. Dnieper   45° N

Graz   **Budapest**   **Chişinău**   Odesa   Kerch   Sea of Azov

HUNGARY   Bacău

ENIA   Pécs   Szeged   Cluj-Napoca   Crimea

iana   **Zagreb**   Timişoara   **ROMANIA**   Braşov   Sevastopol'   3

CROATIA   R. Danube   Novi Sad   Transylvanian Alps   Galaţi

Banja Luka   **BOSNIA-**   Ploieşti   Constanţa   **Black Sea**

Split   **HERZEGOVINA**   **Belgrade**   Craiova   **Bucharest**   R. Danube

Dinaric Alps   **Sarajevo**   **SERBIA**   Ruse   Varna

Dubrovnik   Niš   Balkan Mts   Burgas

MONTENEGRO   **Pristina**   **Sofia**   Zonguldak

Podgorica   **KOSOVO**   **BULGARIA**   Plovdiv   Edirne

Shkodër   **Skopje**   Istanbul   R. Kizilirmak

Bari   **Tirana**   **MACEDONIA**   Bitola   **Ankara**   40° N

ALBANIA   Gallipoli   Bursa   Eskişehir   **TURKEY**

Taranto   Brindisi   Thessaloniki   Çanakkale   Kütahya

Mount Olympus 2911   Pindus Mts   Aegean Sea   Konya

Catanzaro   Ioannina   Larisa   Izmir   Taurus Mountains

Corfu   **GREECE**   Denizli

Reggio di Calabria   Patras   Corinth   **Athens**   Antalya   Alanya   Latakia   Hamāh   35° N

tania   **Ionian Sea**   Kalamata   Rhodes   Homs   **SYRIA**

a   Iraklion   **Nicosia**   Tripoli

Crete   **CYPRUS**   Limassol   **Beirut**   **LEBANON**   **Damascus**

Haifa   Irbid   1

ISRAEL   **Amman**   JORDAN

20° E   25° E   30° E   Tel Aviv-Yafo   **Jerusalem**

Mediterranean Sea

Key to symbols

- ■ Capital city
- ○ Main city/town
- ○ Other city/town
- —— Country boundary
- — Road
- ⊣⊢ Railway
- ⌣ Canal
- ⊕ Airport
- ⬭ Lake
- ⬭ Seasonal lake
- ⌇ River
- ▲ Mont Blanc 4810   Mountain and height in metres

Land height above sea level in metres

over 5000
3000 – 5000
2000 – 3000
1000 – 2000
500 – 1000
200 – 500
0 – 200

Land below sea level

N
W   E
S

Alps divide Europe with a wall of rock and ice 1000 km long.

Capital populations

Millions

7 — Madrid
6 —
5 —
4 — Lisbon   Rome   Athens
3 —
2 — Sofia   Bucharest
1 —
0 —

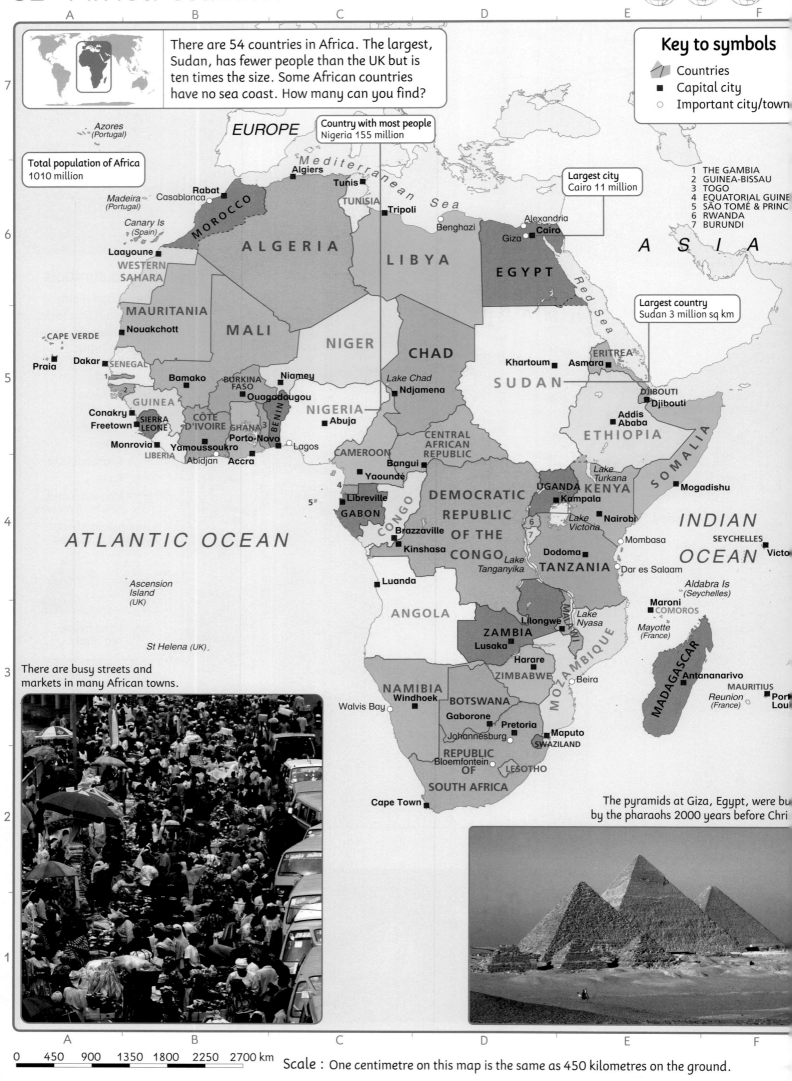

There are 54 countries in Africa. The largest, Sudan, has fewer people than the UK but is ten times the size. Some African countries have no sea coast. How many can you find?

Key to symbols
- Countries
- ■ Capital city
- ○ Important city/town

Country with most people
Nigeria 155 million

Largest city
Cairo 11 million

Total population of Africa
1010 million

Largest country
Sudan 3 million sq km

1 THE GAMBIA
2 GUINEA-BISSAU
3 TOGO
4 EQUATORIAL GUINE
5 SÃO TOMÉ & PRINC
6 RWANDA
7 BURUNDI

EUROPE

*Azores
(Portugal)*

*Madeira
(Portugal)*

*Canary Is
(Spain)*

Mediterranean Sea

Algiers
Tunis
Rabat
Casablanca
Tripoli
MOROCCO
Benghazi
Alexandria
Giza
Cairo
Laayoune
WESTERN SAHARA
ALGERIA
LIBYA
EGYPT
TUNISIA

Red Sea

A S I A

MAURITANIA
MALI
NIGER
CHAD
SUDAN
Khartoum
Asmara
ERITREA
DJIBOUTI
Djibouti

CAPE VERDE
Nouakchott
Praia
Dakar
SENEGAL
Bamako
BURKINA FASO
Niamey
Ouagadougou
Ndjamena
Lake Chad
Addis Ababa
ETHIOPIA

Conakry
GUINEA
Freetown
SIERRA LEONE
CÔTE D'IVOIRE
GHANA
BENIN
NIGERIA
Abuja
Porto-Novo
Lagos
CENTRAL AFRICAN REPUBLIC
Monrovia
LIBERIA
Yamoussoukro
Abidjan
Accra
CAMEROON
Bangui
Yaoundé
Lake Turkana
UGANDA
Kampala
KENYA
Nairobi
SOMALIA
Mogadishu

INDIAN OCEAN

Libreville
GABON
CONGO
DEMOCRATIC REPUBLIC OF THE CONGO
Brazzaville
Kinshasa
Lake Tanganyika
Lake Victoria
Dodoma
TANZANIA
Mombasa
Dar es Salaam
SEYCHELLES
Victo

ATLANTIC OCEAN

*Ascension Island
(UK)*

Luanda

*Aldabra Is
(Seychelles)*

*Mayotte
(France)*

Maroni
COMOROS

St Helena (UK)

ANGOLA
ZAMBIA
Lusaka
MALAWI
Lilongwe
Lake Nyasa
MOZAMBIQUE
MADAGASCAR
Antananarivo
MAURITIUS
Port Lou
*Reunion
(France)*

There are busy streets and markets in many African towns.

Harare
ZIMBABWE
Beira

NAMIBIA
Windhoek
Walvis Bay
BOTSWANA
Gaborone
Pretoria
Johannesburg
Maputo
SWAZILAND
Bloemfontein
REPUBLIC OF
LESOTHO
SOUTH AFRICA
Cape Town

The pyramids at Giza, Egypt, were bu by the pharaohs 2000 years before Chri

A B C D E F

0 450 900 1350 1800 2250 2700 km

Scale : One centimetre on this map is the same as 450 kilometres on the ground.

A B C D E F

Africa lies across the Equator. The Sahara desert stretches across the north. At the Equator there are rainforests. Grasslands and mountains are found in the south and east.

EUROPE

Azores

Total area of Africa
30 million sq km

Madeira

Canary Islands

Mediterranean Sea

Atlas Mountains

Longest river
River Nile 6695 km

ASIA

Sinai

7

6

Cape Verde Islands

S a h a r a

▲ *Ahaggar*
2918

Qattara Depression

Libyan Desert

Lake Nasser

R. Nile

Red Sea

R. Sénégal

R. Niger

▲ *Tibesti*
3415

R. Niger

R. Benue

Lake Chad

R. Blue Nile

R. White Nile

Ras Dejen
4533 ▲

Lake Tana

Ethiopian Highlands

Lake Assal

Gulf of Aden

Lowest point
Lake Assal
156 metres below sea level

5

Lake Volta

Gulf of Guinea

Bioco

São Tomé

Key to symbols

Land height above
sea level in metres

over 5000
2000 – 5000
1000 – 2000
500 – 1000
200 – 500
0 – 200

Kilimanjaro
5892 ▲ Mountain and
height in metres

River

Lake

Land below
sea level

R. Ubangi

R. Congo

R. Congo

Congo Basin

R. Congo

Margherita Peak
5110 ▲

Lake Victoria

Kilimanjaro ▲
5892

Mount Kenya
5199 ▲

Webi Shabeelle

Lake Turkana

INDIAN

OCEAN

Largest lake
Lake Victoria 68 800 sq km

4

ATLANTIC

OCEAN

St Helena

Lake Tanganyika

Great Rift Valley

Aldabra Islands

Comoro Islands

Mayotte

Lake Nyasa

Mauritius

Reunion

Madagascar

3

The Victoria Falls on the River Zambezi are nearly two kilometres wide and form the longest curtain of water in the world.

Bie Plateau

Namib Desert

R. Zambezi

Okavango Delta

Victoria Falls

R. Zambezi

R. Limpopo

K a l a h a r i D e s e r t

R. Orange

R. Vaal

Drakensberg

Mozambique Channel

Largest island
Madagascar 587 040 sq km

2

Cape of Good Hope

A Bedouin nomad in the Sahara Desert with his camels.

A B C D E F

450 900 1350 1800 2250 2700 km

Scale : One centimetre on this map is the same as 450 kilometres on the ground.

Egypt is one of the oldest countries in the world. Today it has a population of 83 million. Most people live in the valley of the River Nile. The capital, Cairo, is larger than London.

Facts about Egypt

Area..................... 1 million sq km
Highest Peak... Jabal Katrina 2637 m
Longest river............. Nile 6695 km
Largest lake..... L. Nasser 5248 sq km
Population................... 83 million
Largest city............Cairo 11 million

SYRIA

JORDAN

Mediterranean Sea

Haifa
Sea of Galilee
Irbid
Tel Aviv-Yafo
WEST BANK
Amman
Jerusalem
Dead Sea
GAZA
Beersheba
ISRAEL
Negev
Eilat
Aqaba
Tabuk

SAUDI

ARABIA

Umm Sa'ad
Marsa Matruh
Libyan Plateau
Dumyat
Port Said
Alexandria
Damanhur
Tanta
Al Isma'iliyah
Giza
Cairo
Suez
Suez Canal
Al Jaghbub
Qattara Depression
Siwah
Al Fayyum
Bani Suwayf
R. Nile
Eastern Desert
Sinai
Jabal Katrina 2637
Gulf of Suez
Al Ghurdaqah
Duba

LIBYA

Great Sand Sea

Al Bawiti
Bahariya Oasis
Al Minya
Qasr Farafra
Farafra Oasis
Western Desert
EGYPT
Asyut
Sawhaj
Qina
Luxor
Al Kharijah
Mut Dakhla Oasis
The Great Oasis
Idfu
Bur Safajah
Al Qusayr
Al Wajh
Marsa al'Alam
H i j a z
Red Sea

Libyan Desert

Tropic of Cancer
Hadabat al Jilf al Kabir
Aswan
Lake Nasser
Bi'r Shalatayn
Al 'Uwaynat
Lake Nuba
Wadi Halfa
Abu Sunbul
N u b i a n Desert
Jedd

Nile Delta

Red Sea

Sahara

This satellite image shows the river Nile as it threads across the desert. Note the way the valley fans out into a delta as the Nile reaches the sea.

Kerma
Ed Debba
R. Nile
SUDAN
Port Sudan

N
W E
S

Key to symbols

- ■ Capital city
- ○ Main city/town
- ○ Other city/town
- ▬ Country boundary
- ▬ Road
- ▬ Railway
- ∿ Canal
- ⊕ Airport
- Lake
- Seasonal lake
- ～ River
- *Jabal Katrina* ▲ 2637 Mountain and height in metres

Land height above sea level in metres

over 5000
3000 – 5000
2000 – 3000
1000 – 2000
500 – 1000
200 – 500
0 – 200

Land below sea level

0 100 200 300 400 500 km

Scale : One centimetre on this map is the same as 75 kilometres on the ground.

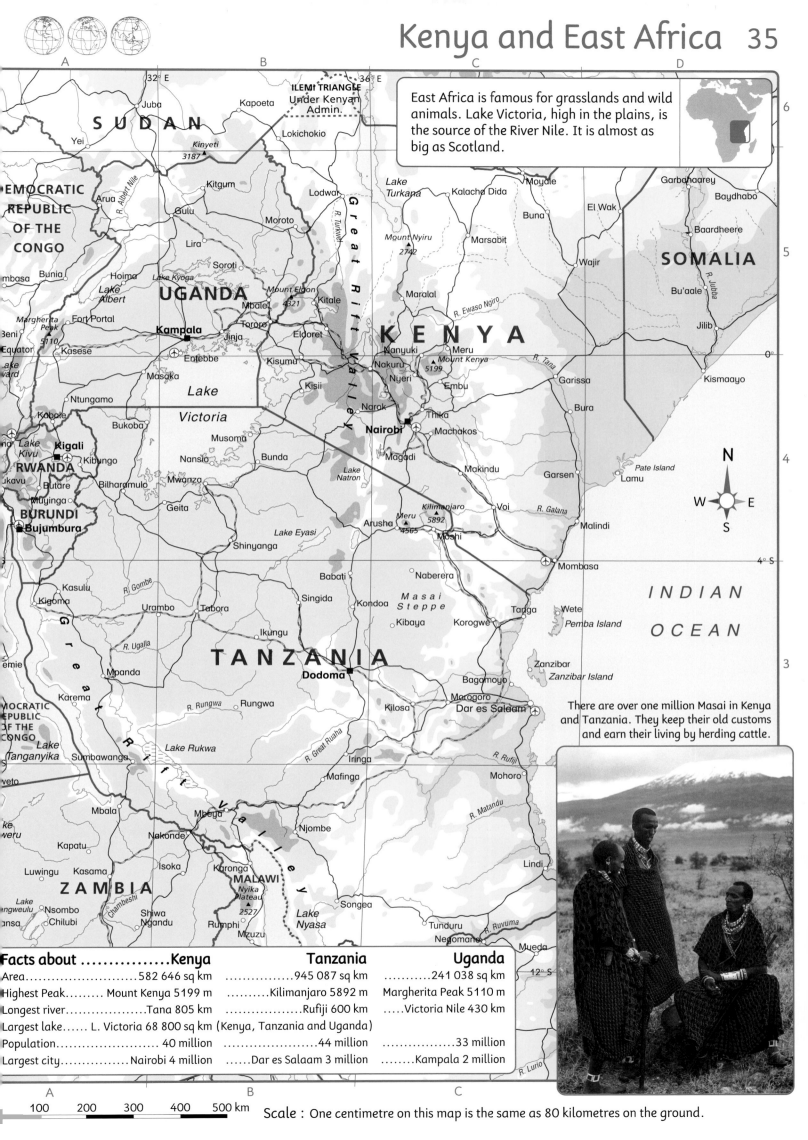

A · B · 32 E · 36 E · C · D

6

SUDAN

Juba
Kapoeta
Yei
Kinyeti 3187
Kitgum
Lokichokio

ILEMI TRIANGLE
Under Kenyan Admin.

East Africa is famous for grasslands and wild animals. Lake Victoria, high in the plains, is the source of the River Nile. It is almost as big as Scotland.

DEMOCRATIC REPUBLIC OF THE CONGO

Arua
R. Albert Nile
Gulu
Lira
Soroti
Moroto
Lodwar
Lake Turkana
Kalacha Dida
Moyale
Garbahaarey
Baydhabo

mbasa
Bunia
Hoima
Lake Albert
Lake Kyoga
UGANDA
Mount Elgon 4321
Kitale
Maralal
Mount Nyiru 2742
Marsabit
Buna
El Wak
Baardheere

SOMALIA

Margherita Peak 5110
Beni
Equator
Fort Portal
Kampala
Jinja
Tororo
Eldoret
Kisumu
Nanyuki
Meru
Mount Kenya 5199
Wajir
Bu'aale
Jilib
0°

Kasese
Entebbe
KENYA
Nakuru
Nyeri
Embu
R. Tana
Garissa
Kismaayo

Kaward
Lake
Kobale
Masaka
Ntungamo
Bukoba
Lake Victoria
Kisii
Narok
Nairobi
Thika
Machakos
Bura
Garsen
Lamu
Pate Island

Kigali
RWANDA
Kibungo
Musoma
Nansio
Bunda
Magadi
Makindu
N
4

Rukavu
Butare
Bilharamulo
Mwanza
Geita
Lake Natron
Meru 4565
Kilimanjaro 5892
Voi
R. Galana
Malindi
W   E

Muyinga
BURUNDI
Bujumbura
Shinyanga
Lake Eyasi
Arusha
Moshi
S

INDIAN

Great Rift Valley

Kigoma
Kasulu
R. Gombe
Urambo
Tabora
Babati
Naberera
Masai Steppe
Mombasa
4° S
OCEAN

emie
Mpanda
R. Ugalla
Ikungu
Singida
Kondoa
Kibaya
Korogwe
Tanga
Wete
Pemba Island

Karema
TANZANIA
Dodoma
Kilosa
Bagamoyo
Zanzibar
Zanzibar Island
3

DEMOCRATIC REPUBLIC OF THE CONGO
Lake Tanganyika
Sumbawanga
R. Rungwa
Rungwa
Morogoro
Dar es Salaam

There are over one million Masai in Kenya and Tanzania. They keep their old customs and earn their living by herding cattle.

veto
Lake Rukwa
R. Great Ruaha
Iringa
R. Rufiji

Mbala
Mbeya
Mafinga
Mohoro

weru
Nakonde
Njombe
R. Matandu

Kapatu
Isoka
Lindi

Luwingu
Kasama
Karonga
MALAWI
Nyika Plateau 2527
ZAMBIA
Chambeshi
Songea
Tunduru
Negomano
12° S

Lake ngweulu
Nsombo
Chilubi
ansa
Shiwa Ngandu
Rumphi
Mzuzu
Lake Nyasa
R. Ruvuma
Mueda
R. Lurio

Facts about .... Kenya · Tanzania · Uganda

	Kenya	Tanzania	Uganda
Area	582 646 sq km	945 087 sq km	241 038 sq km
Highest Peak	Mount Kenya 5199 m	Kilimanjaro 5892 m	Margherita Peak 5110 m
Longest river	Tana 805 km	Rufiji 600 km	Victoria Nile 430 km
Largest lake	L. Victoria 68 800 sq km (Kenya, Tanzania and Uganda)		
Population	40 million	44 million	33 million
Largest city	Nairobi 4 million	Dar es Salaam 3 million	Kampala 2 million

A · B · C

100   200   300   400   500 km

Scale : One centimetre on this map is the same as 80 kilometres on the ground.

There are 49 countries in Asia. India, China and the Russian Federation are the largest. Singapore is the smallest. Some are islands. See how many you can find on the map.

Country with most people
China 1330 million

Largest country
Russian Federation 17 million sq km

Russian Federation
Area 17 million sq km
Population 141 million

Total population of Asia
(including Russian Federation)
4262 million

Largest city
Tokyo 37 million

ARCTIC OCEAN

EUROPE

RUSSIAN FEDERATION

St Petersburg
Moscow
Perm
Chelyabinsk
Omsk
Novosibirsk
Volgograd
Yakutsk

Sea of Okhotsk
Sakhalin

Black Sea
Ankara
TURKEY
CYPRUS
LEBANON
ISRAEL
SYRIA
JORDAN
IRAQ
Baghdad
KUWAIT
Kuwait
Tehran
IRAN
Riyadh
SAUDI ARABIA
BAHRAIN
QATAR
UNITED ARAB EMIRATES
OMAN
Muscat
San'a
YEMEN
Aden
Red Sea

KAZAKHSTAN
Astana
Aral Sea
Lake Balkhash
Almaty
Tashkent
UZBEKISTAN
TURKMENISTAN
Ashgabat
Caspian Sea
Ürümqi

Irkutsk
Lake Baikal

MONGOLIA
Ulan Bator

Harbin
Shenyang
Sapporo
Sea of Japan (East Sea)
JAPAN
Tokyo
Kobe
Osaka
Fukuoka

NORTH KOREA
Pyongyang
Beijing
Tianjin
SOUTH KOREA
Seoul

Lanzhou
Xi'an
Nanjing
Shanghai
Wuhan

Kabul
AFGHANISTAN
Islamabad
Lahore
PAKISTAN
Delhi
New Delhi
Karachi

CHINA
Chongqing
Guangzhou
Hong Kong

T'aipei
TAIWAN
PACIFIC OCEAN

NEPAL
BHUTAN
BANGLADESH
Dhaka
INDIA
Kolkata
MYANMAR (BURMA)
Nay Pyi Taw
Yangon
Hanoi
Vientiane
LAOS
VIETNAM
THAILAND
Bangkok
CAMBODIA
Phnom Penh
Ho Chi Minh City

Mumbai
Hyderabad
Chennai

Arabian Sea

Socotra (Yemen)

AFRICA

Bay of Bengal

Andaman Is (India)

South China Sea
Manila
PHILIPPINES
Luzon
Mindanao
Davao

1 GEORGIA
2 ARMENIA
3 AZERBAIJAN
4 TAJIKISTAN
5 KYRGYZSTAN

SRI LANKA
Sri Jayewardenepura Kotte
Colombo
MALDIVES

Nicobar Is (India)

BRUNEI
MALAYSIA
Kuala Lumpur
SINGAPORE
Putrajaya
Sumatra
Borneo
Celebes
Makassar
INDONESIA
Jakarta
Java
Surabaya
Dili
EAST TIMOR

INDIAN OCEAN

AUSTRALIA

Half the people in the world live in Asia, many of them in India and China.

Key to symbols

- Countries
- ■ Capital city
- ○ Important city/town

In the centre of Asia, the Himalayas form the largest mountain range in the world. The Gobi desert and forests of Siberia lie to the north. Southeast Asia is dotted with islands.

Total area of Asia
5 million sq km

Largest lake
Caspian Sea 371 000 sq km

Lowest point
Dead Sea
420 metres below
sea level

ARCTIC OCEAN

EUROPE

Ural Mountains

West Siberian Plain

Central Siberian Plateau

Siberia

R. Yenisey

R. Ob

R. Lena

R. Angara

R. Lena

R. Amur

R. Argun

Sea of Okhotsk

Sakhalin

Hokkaido

Black Sea

Caucasus

Caspian Lowland

Caspian Sea

Aral Sea

Lake Balkhash

R. Irtysh

R. Yenisey

Lake Baikal

R. Selenga

Altai Mts

Sea of Japan (East Sea)

Honshu

Elburz Mountains

Dead Sea

R. Euphrates

R. Tigris

Zagros Mountains

The Gulf

Ysyk-Köl

Tien Shan

Tarim Basin

Hindu Kush

K2 8611

Kunlun Shan

Plateau of Tibet

Gobi Desert

Huang He

Kyushu

East China Sea

Longest river
Chang Jiang 6380 km

Red Sea

Arabian Peninsula

R. Indus

Thar Desert

Himalaya

Annapurna 8091

Mount Everest 8848

R. Ganges

Chang Jiang

R. Irrawaddy

Taiwan

PACIFIC OCEAN

Gulf of Aden

AFRICA

Arabian Sea

Deccan

Bay of Bengal

Highest mountain
Mount Everest 8848 m

R. Mekong

Luzon

Philippines

South China Sea

Mindanao

Sri Lanka

This satellite image shows the delta of the River Ganges in Bangladesh. This is one of the most densely populated areas in the world.

Sumatra

Borneo

Celebes

Java

INDIAN OCEAN

Largest island
Borneo 745 561 sq km

AUSTRALIA

BANGLADESH

Bay of Bengal

Key to symbols

Land height above sea level in metres

over 5000
2000 – 5000
1000 – 2000
500 – 1000
200 – 500
0 – 200

Mount Everest 8848
Mountain and height in metres

River
Lake
Seasonal lake
Ice cap
Land below sea level

500 1000 1500 2000 2500 3000 3500 4000 km

Scale : One centimetre on this map is the same as 500 kilometres on the ground.

Africa, Asia and Europe join together in the Middle East. Many ancient civilizations grew up here. Today, the differences between people and religions have led to terrible conflicts.

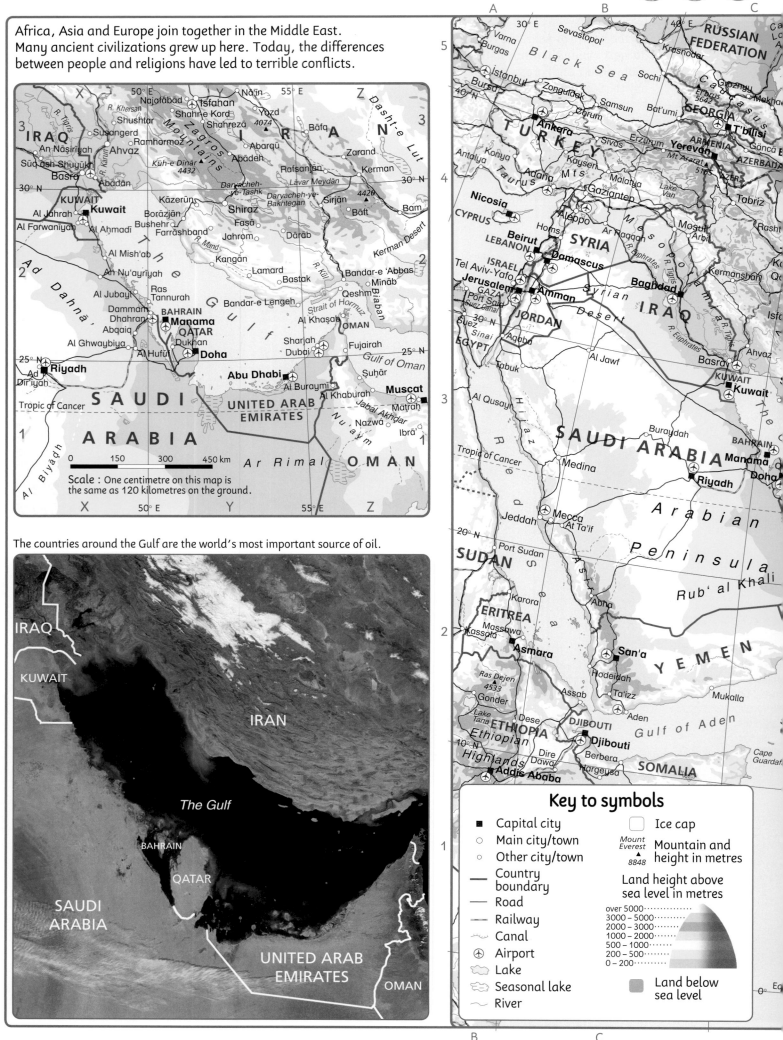

Scale : One centimetre on this map is the same as 120 kilometres on the ground.

The countries around the Gulf are the world's most important source of oil.

Key to symbols

- ■ Capital city
- ○ Main city/town
- ○ Other city/town
- — Country boundary
- — Road
- — Railway
- — Canal
- ✈ Airport
- Lake
- Seasonal lake
- River

- ☐ Ice cap
- *Mount Everest* ▲ Mountain and height in metres
  8848

Land height above sea level in metres

- over 5000
- 3000 – 5000
- 2000 – 3000
- 1000 – 2000
- 500 – 1000
- 200 – 500
- 0 – 200

Land below sea level

0 200 400 600 800 1000 1200 km

Scale : One centimetre on this map is the same as 200 kilometres on the ground.

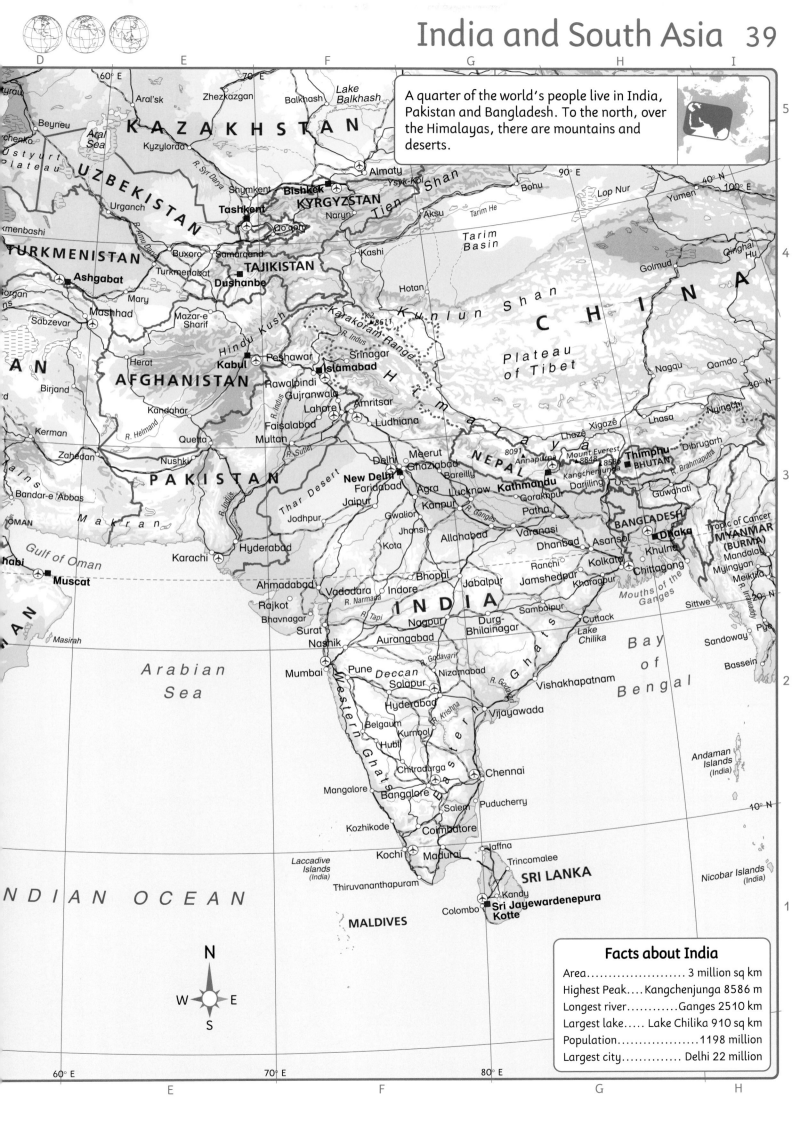

A quarter of the world's people live in India, Pakistan and Bangladesh. To the north, over the Himalayas, there are mountains and deserts.

KAZAKHSTAN

Aral'sk
Zhezkazgan
Balkhash
Lake Balkhash
Beyneu
Almaty
Ysyk-Kol
Tien Shan
Bohu
Yumen
Aral Sea
Kyzylorda
Shymkent
Bishkek
KYRGYZSTAN
Naryn
Aksu
Tarim He
Lop Nur
Ückchenko
Üstyurt Plateau
R. Syr Darya
Tashkent
Qo'qon
Tarim Basin
Qinghai Hu
UZBEKISTAN
Urganch
Buxoro
Samarqand
Kashi
Hotan
Golmud
Kunlun Shan
CHINA
menbashi
R. Amu Darya
Turkmenabat
TAJIKISTAN
Dushanbe
K2 8611
Karakoram Range
R. Indus
TURKMENISTAN
Ashgabat
Mary
Mazar-e Sharif
Hindu Kush
Peshawar
Srinagar
Plateau of Tibet
Nagqu
Qamdo
Mashhad
Herat
Kabul
Islamabad
Rawalpindi
Himalaya
Lhazê
Xigazê
Lhasa
Nyingchi
Sabzevar
Birjand
AFGHANISTAN
Gujranwala
Amritsar
8091
Annapurna
Mount Everest 8848
Dibrugarh
Kerman
Kandahar
R. Helmand
Quetta
Lahore
Ludhiana
NEPAL
Kangchenjunga 8586
Thimphu
Guwahati
Zahedan
Nushki
Multan
R. Sutlej
Delhi
Meerut
Annapurna
Kathmandu
BHUTAN
R. Brahmaputra
Bandar-e Abbas
PAKISTAN
Ghaziabad
Bareilly
Darjiling
Nashik
New Delhi
Faridabad
Agra
Lucknow
Gorakhpur
Patna
BANGLADESH
Gulf of Oman
Makran
R. Indus
Thar Desert
Jaipur
Kanpur
R. Ganges
Dhanbad
Asansol
Dhaka
Tropic of Cancer
MYANMAR (BURMA)
Muscat
Jodhpur
Gwalior
Jhansi
Allahabad
Varanasi
Ranchi
Khulna
Chittagong
Mandalay
Hyderabad
Kota
Bhopal
Jabalpur
Jamshedpur
Kharagpur
Kolkata
Mouths of the Ganges
Myingyan
Meiktila
Ahmadabad
Indore
INDIA
Durg-Bhilainagar
Sambalpur
Cuttack
Lake Chilika
Sittwe
Rajkot
Vadodara
R. Narmada
Nagpur
Sandoway
Bhavnagar
R. Tapi
Aurangabad
Nizamabad
R. Godavari
Vishakhapatnam
Bay of Bengal
Bassein
Surat
Mumbai
Pune
Deccan
Solapur
R. Godavari
Masirah
Arabian Sea
Hyderabad
R. Krishna
Vijayawada
Belgaum
Kurnool
Western Ghats
Andaman Islands (India)
Hubli
Chitradurga
Chennai
Mangalore
Bangalore
Salem
Puducherry
Kozhikode
Coimbatore
Kochi
Madurai
Jaffna
Trincomalee
Nicobar Islands (India)
Laccadive Islands (India)
SRI LANKA
Thiruvananthapuram
Kandy
INDIAN OCEAN
Colombo
Sri Jayewardenepura Kotte
MALDIVES

N
W E
S

Facts about India

Area........................ 3 million sq km
Highest Peak....Kangchenjunga 8586 m
Longest river............Ganges 2510 km
Largest lake..... Lake Chilika 910 sq km
Population...................1198 million
Largest city............. Delhi 22 million

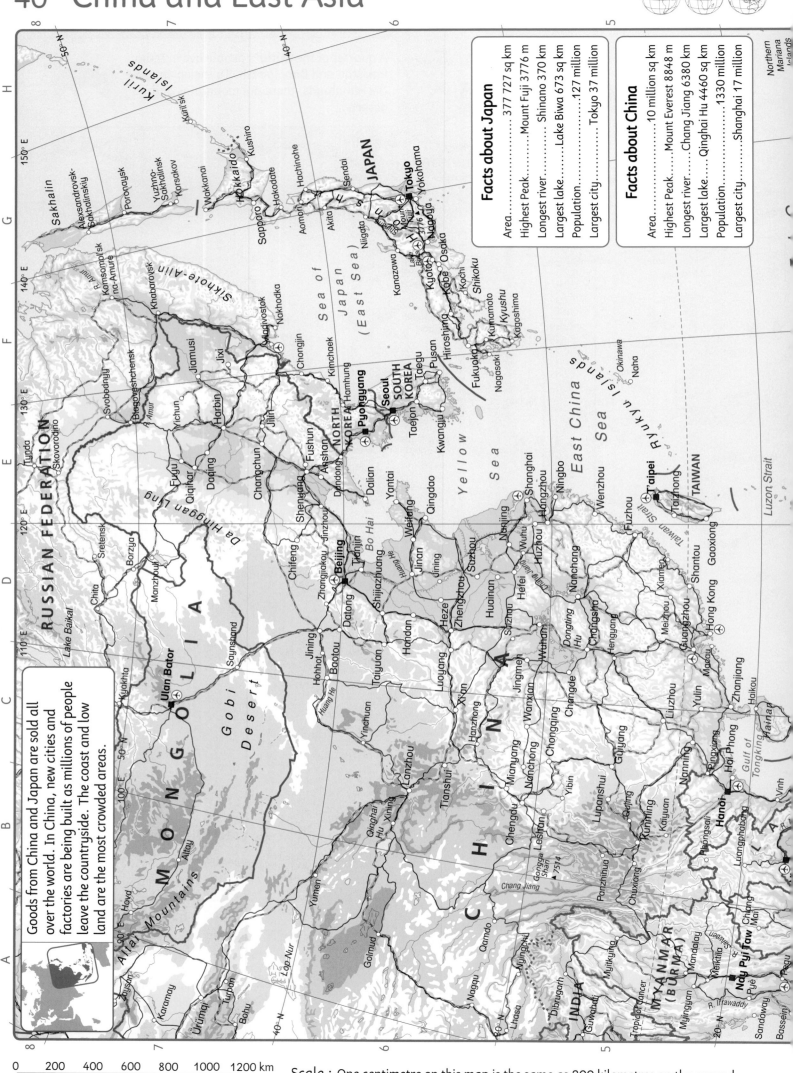

Facts about Japan

Area................................377 727 sq km
Highest Peak.......Mount Fuji 3776 m
Longest river...............Shinano 370 km
Largest lake.........Lake Biwa 673 sq km
Population.............................127 million
Largest city...............Tokyo 37 million

Facts about China

Area................................10 million sq km
Highest Peak.....Mount Everest 8848 m
Longest river.......Chang Jiang 6380 km
Largest lake........Qinghai Hu 4460 sq km
Population.............................1330 million
Largest city...............Shanghai 17 million

Goods from China and Japan are sold all over the world. In China, new cities and factories are being built as millions of people leave the countryside. The coast and low land are the most crowded areas.

Scale : One centimetre on this map is the same as 200 kilometres on the ground.

0   200   400   600   800   1000   1200 km

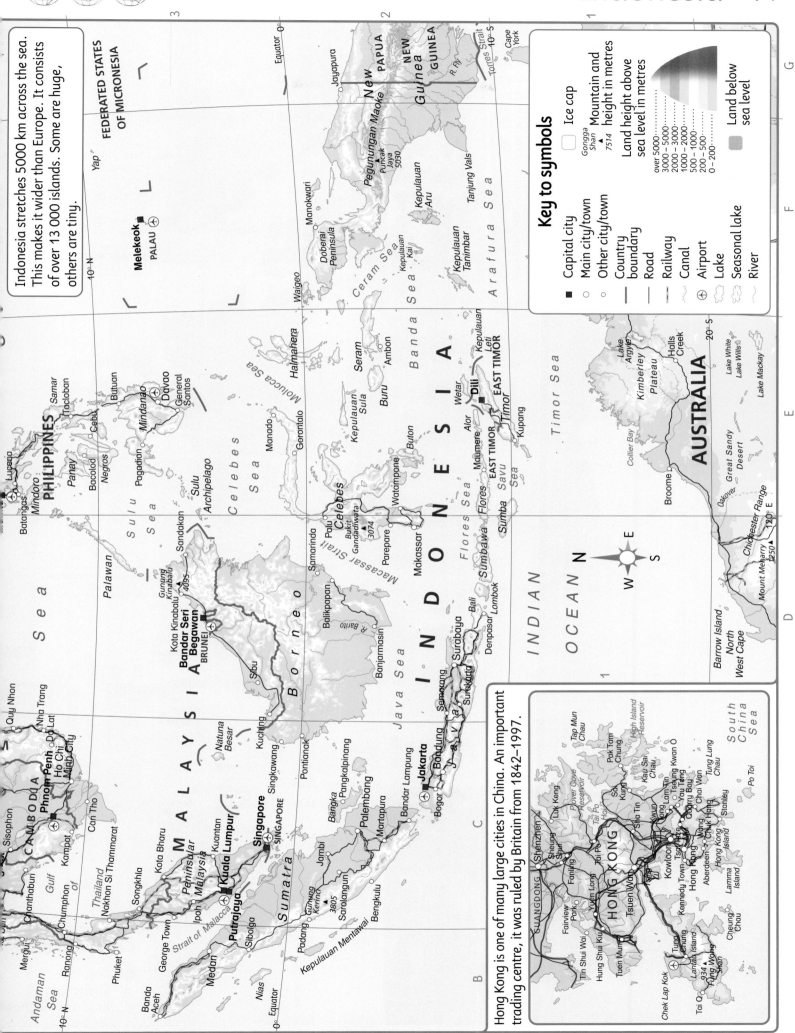

Canada, Mexico and the USA make up most of North America. Many small countries are found in the narrow belt of land which leads to South America and in the Caribbean Sea.

ARCTIC OCEAN

GREENLAND
(Denmark)

Baffin Bay

ALASKA
U.S.A.

Anchorage

Nuuk
(Godthåb)

Iqaluit

Total population of North America
539 million

Largest country
Canada 10 million sq km

Great Bear Lake

Great Slave Lake

Hudson Bay

C A N A D A

St John's

Edmonton

Vancouver

Calgary

Quebec

Montreal

Halifax

Seattle

Winnipeg

Lake Huron

Ottawa

PACIFIC OCEAN

Portland

Lake Superior

Toronto

Lake Ontario

Boston

Minneapolis

Lake Michigan

Detroit

Lake Erie

New York

ATLANTIC OCEAN

Chicago

Pittsburgh

Washington D.C.

Sacramento

U N I T E D   S T A T E S

St Louis

San Francisco

Salt Lake City

Denver

Kansas City

O F   A M E R I C A

Bermuda (UK)

Los Angeles

San Diego

Phoenix

Country with most people
USA 315 million

El Paso

Dallas

Atlanta

Houston

New Orleans

Miami

THE BAHAMAS

ANTIGUA & BARBUD

Nassau

Monterrey

Gulf of Mexico

Havana

CUBA

HAITI

DOMINICAN REPUBLIC

PUERTO RICO
(USA)

DOMINICA

ST LUCI

BAR

Largest city
Mexico City 20 million

M E X I C O

JAMAICA

Kingston

GRENAD

Guadalajara

Caribbean Sea

Mexico City

Puebla

BELIZE

Manhattan in the centre of New York is a centre for business and entertainment.

HONDURAS

GUATEMALA

NICARAGUA

Guatemala City

EL SALVADOR

Managua

Panama City

COSTA RICA

PANAMA

SOUTH

AMERICA

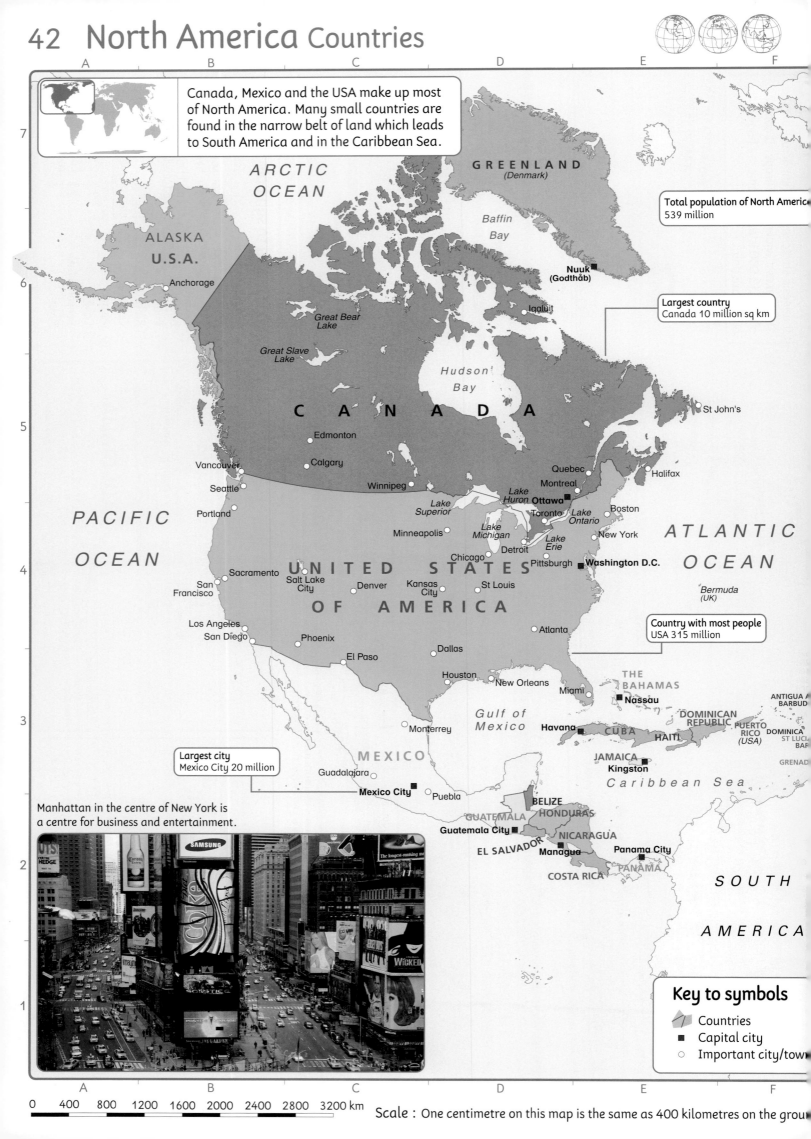

Key to symbols

- Countries
- ■ Capital city
- ○ Important city/tow

Scale : One centimetre on this map is the same as 400 kilometres on the grou

The Rocky Mountains stretch down the western side of North America. Further east there are lakes and plains. In the north, Greenland is covered in ice.

ARCTIC OCEAN

PACIFIC OCEAN

ATLANTIC OCEAN

Greenland

Baffin Bay

Davis Strait

Cape Farewell

Ellesmere Island

Baffin Island

Victoria Island

R. Yukon

Mount McKinley 6194

Gulf of Alaska

Mount Logan 5959

R. Mackenzie

Great Bear Lake

Great Slave Lake

Coast Mountains

R. Peace

Hudson Bay

Labrador

Newfoundland

Canadian Shield

R. St Lawrence

Rocky Mountains

3954

Great Plains

Lake Superior

Great Lakes

Lake Huron

Lake Ontario

Cape Cod

Niagara Falls

Lake Michigan

Lake Erie

R. Snake

R. Missouri

R. North Platte

Mount Elbert 4398

Appalachian Mountains

2037

Great Salt Lake

Great Basin

Death Valley

Grand Canyon

R. Colorado

Mount Whitney 4418

R. Red

R. Ohio

R. Mississippi

Gulf of California

Sierra Madre Occidental

Sierra Madre Oriental

R. Brazos

Rio Grande

Gulf of Mexico

Florida

Cuba

Hispaniola

Caribbean Sea

Yucatán

Popocatépetl 5452

Lake Nicaragua

Isthmus of Panama

SOUTH AMERICA

Total area of North America
25 million sq km

Largest island
Greenland 2 million sq km

Largest lake
Lake Superior 82 100 sq km

Highest mountain
Mount McKinley 6194 m

Lowest point
Death Valley 86 metres below sea level

Longest river
Mississippi-Missouri 5969 km

Key to symbols

Land height above sea level in metres

over 5000
2000 – 5000
1000 – 2000
500 – 1000
200 – 500
0 – 200

Mount McKinley 6194 ▲ Mountain and height in metres

River

Lake

Seasonal lake

Ice cap

Land below sea level

The Grand Canyon on the Colorado River is 1500 metres deep and over 400 km long. It was one of the first National Parks in the USA.

400 800 1200 1600 2000 2400 2800 3200 km

Scale : One centimetre on this map is the same as 400 kilometres on the ground.

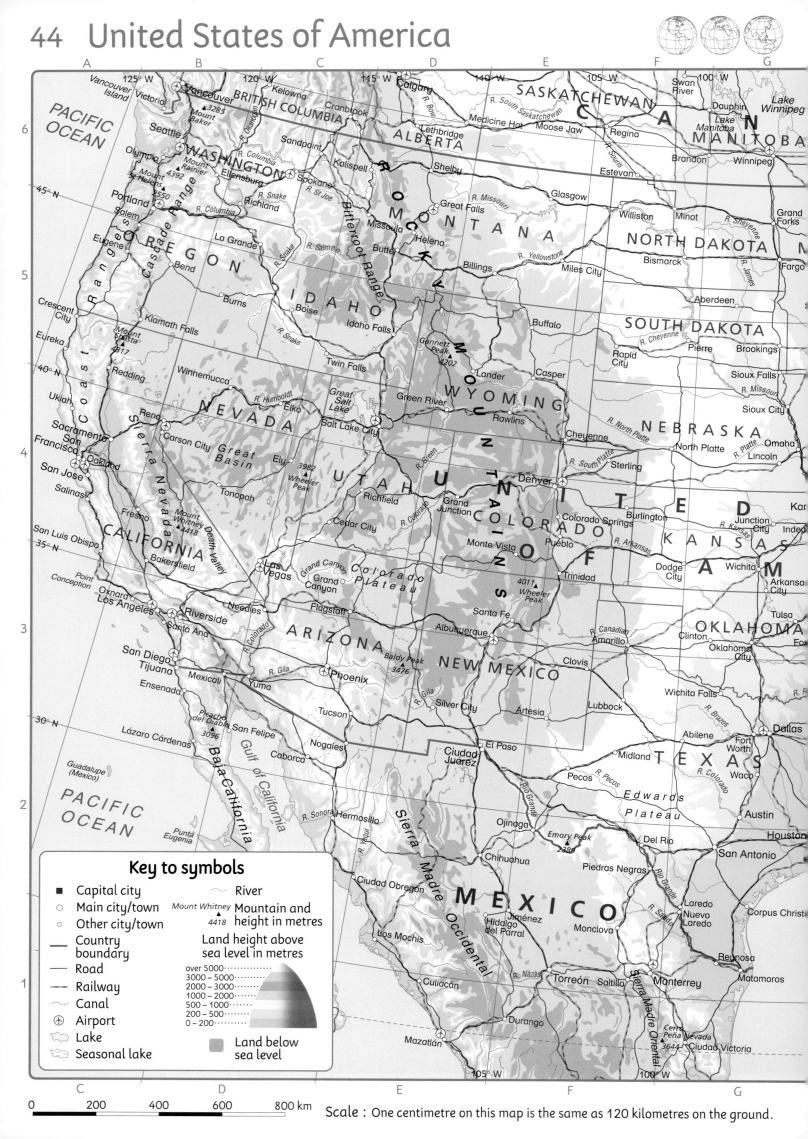

Key to symbols

- ■ Capital city
- ○ Main city/town
- ○ Other city/town
- —— Country boundary
- —— Road
- —— Railway
- ～～ Canal
- ⊕ Airport
- Lake
- Seasonal lake

- ～ River
- *Mount Whitney* ▲ 4418 Mountain and height in metres

Land height above sea level in metres

over 5000
3000 – 5000
2000 – 3000
1000 – 2000
500 – 1000
200 – 500
0 – 200

Land below sea level

Scale : One centimetre on this map is the same as 120 kilometres on the ground.

0   200   400   600   800 km

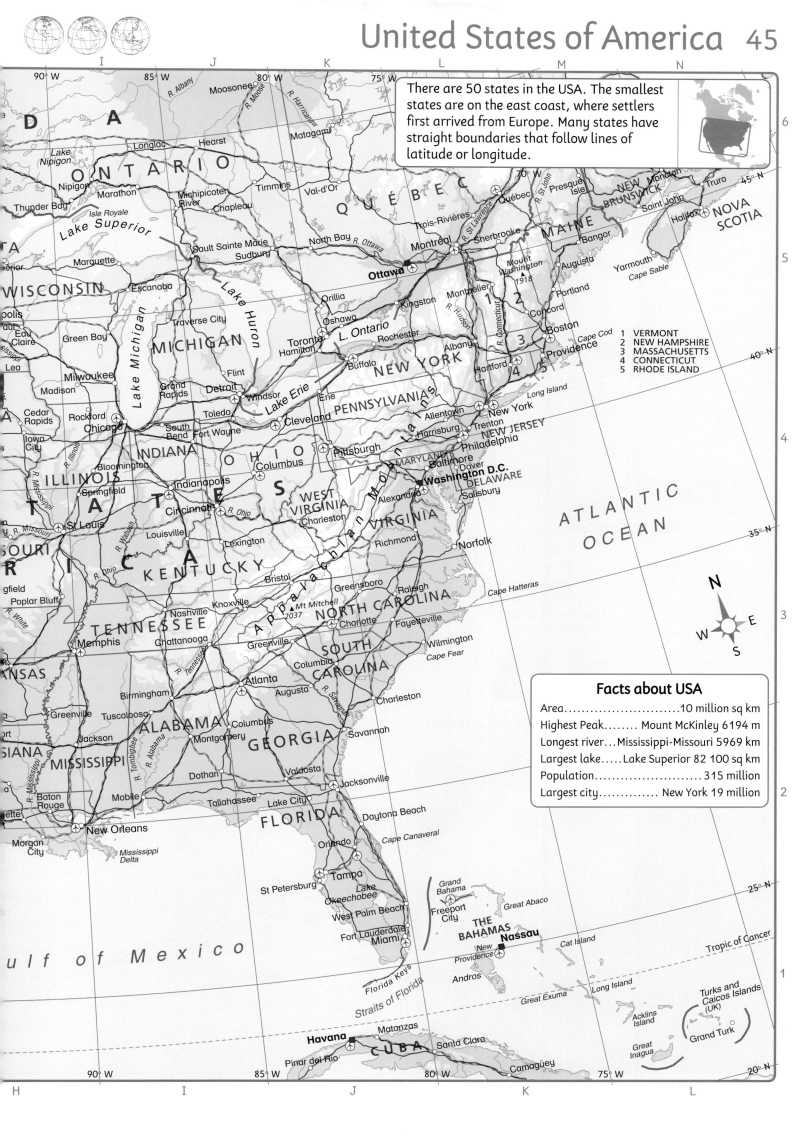

There are 50 states in the USA. The smallest states are on the east coast, where settlers first arrived from Europe. Many states have straight boundaries that follow lines of latitude or longitude.

1 VERMONT
2 NEW HAMPSHIRE
3 MASSACHUSETTS
4 CONNECTICUT
5 RHODE ISLAND

Facts about USA

Area.........................10 million sq km
Highest Peak........ Mount McKinley 6194 m
Longest river...Mississippi-Missouri 5969 km
Largest lake.....Lake Superior 82 100 sq km
Population.........................315 million
Largest city............. New York 19 million

Key to symbols

- ■ Capital city
- ○ Main city/town
- ○ Other city/town
- ▬ Country boundary
- — Road
- ▬ Railway
- ∿ Canal
- ⊕ Airport
- ⎈ Lake
- ⎈ Seasonal lake
- ∿ River
- *Popocatépetl* ▲ Mountain and height in metres
  5452

Land height above sea level in metres

over 5000
3000 – 5000
2000 – 3000
1000 – 2000
500 – 1000
200 – 500
0 – 200

Hurricane Katrina destroyed New Orleans in August 2005. The centre of the storm shows up clearly in this photograph from the air.

Tracks of major hurricanes

- Gordon 1
- Fran 1996
- Mitch 199
- Floyd 199
- Isabel 20
- Charley 2
- Katrina 2
- Rita 2005
- Dean 200

Scale : One centimetre on this map is the same as 135 kilometres on the ground.

0   200   400   600   800 km

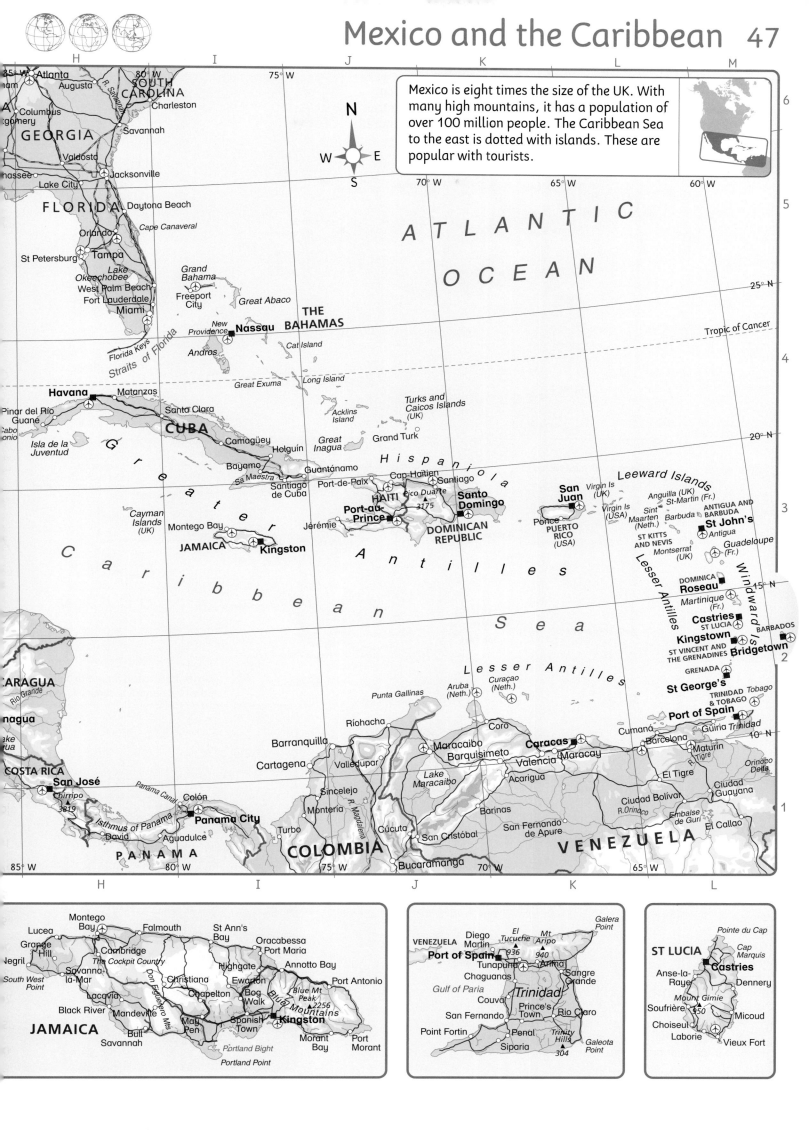

Mexico is eight times the size of the UK. With many high mountains, it has a population of over 100 million people. The Caribbean Sea to the east is dotted with islands. These are popular with tourists.

Brazil covers nearly half of South America. Argentina and Peru area also large countries. Chile is 4000 km long but only a few hundred kilometres wide.

NORTH AMERICA

Barranquilla
Maracaibo
Caracas
Port of Spain
TRINIDAD AND TOBAGO

Medellín

VENEZUELA

Georgetown

GUYANA

Paramaribo
SURINAME

Cayenne

FRENCH GUIANA

Bogotá
COLOMBIA

Cali

Quito
ECUADOR

Galapagos Islands (Ecuador)

Guayaquil

Iquitos

Manaus

Belém

São Luís

Fortaleza

B R A Z I L

Natal

Trujillo

PERU

Recife

Lima

Aracaju

Salvador

Lake Titicaca

BOLIVIA

Brasília

La Paz

Arequipa

Sucre

Largest city
São Paulo 20 million

Belo Horizonte

Antofagasta

PARAGUAY
Asunción

São Paulo

Rio de Janeiro

Largest country
Brazil 9 million sq km

Country with most people
Brazil 194 million

Curitiba

ATLANTIC OCEAN

A R G E N T I N A

Porto Alegre

Juan Fernandez Islands (Chile)

Valparaíso

Santiago

URUGUAY

Buenos Aires

Montevideo

Concepción

Mar del Plata

PACIFIC OCEAN

Falkland Islands (UK)

Rio de Janeiro is a huge city built around o of the best natural harbours in South Americ

Punta Arenas

Tierra del Fuego

Total population of South America
390 million

Key to symbols

- ◢ Countries
- ■ Capital city
- ○ Important city/town

Scale : One centimetre on this map is the same as 400 kilometres on the grou

The Andes, which run down the western edge of South America, are the world's longest chain of mountains. From here the river Amazon flows east to the Atlantic Ocean.

Caribbean Sea

NORTH AMERICA

Lake Maracaibo

R. Orinoco

Orinoco Delta

Angel Falls

Mount Roraima 2810

Guiana Highlands

Llanos

R. Japurá

R. Negro

R. Amazon

Mouths of the Amazon

Galapagos Islands

R. Amazon

A m a z o n B a s i n

S e l v a s

R. Madeira

R. Purus

Longest river
River Amazon 6516 km

R. Tocantins

R. São Francisco

Largest lake
Lake Titicaca 8340 sq km

A n d e s

Altiplano

Lake Titicaca

Atacama Desert

Planalto do Mato Grosso

B r a z i l i a n

H i g h l a n d s

R. Paraguay

PACIFIC OCEAN

Highest mountain
Aconcagua 6959 m

Nevado Ojos del Salado 6908

Gran Chaco

R. Salado

R. Paraná

R. Paraná

R. Uruguay

ATLANTIC OCEAN

Total area of South America
18 million sq km

Aconcagua 6959

Juan Fernandez Islands

P a m p a s

Río de la Plata

R. Colorado

Key to symbols

Land height above sea level in metres

over 5000
2000 – 5000
1000 – 2000
500 – 1000
200 – 500
0 – 200

Land below sea level

Aconcagua 6959   Mountain and height in metres

River

Lake

Seasonal lake

R. Negro

Valdes Peninsula

Isla de Chiloé

Patagonia

Lowest point
Laguna del Carbon 105m below sea level

Falkland Islands

Tierra del Fuego

South Georgia

Largest island
Tierra del Fuego 47 000 sq km

Cape Horn

In South America large areas of rainforest have been cleared for farming. The forest at the bottom of this photograph was saved because it is a National Park.

In South America many people live in towns and cities. The coast is the most crowded. The mountains and other inland areas are much emptier.

N
W E
S

ATLANTIC OCEAN

Caribbean Sea

Lesser Antilles

DOMINICA
ST LUCIA
ST VINCENT & THE GRENADINES
BARBADOS
GRENADA
TRINIDAD & TOBAGO
Port Of Spain

Aruba (Neth.)
Curaçao (Neth.)
Martinique (Fr.)

NICARAGUA
COSTA RICA
PANAMA
Panama City

VENEZUELA
Caracas
Valencia
Maracay
Barquisimeto
Maracaibo
Lake Maracaibo
Coro
Barranquilla
Cartagena
Sincelejo
Monteria
Barinas
Acarigua
Maturin
Barcelona
Güiria
Ciudad Bolívar
Ciudad Guayana
R. Orinoco
Orinoco Delta

GUYANA
Georgetown
SURINAME
Paramaribo
FRENCH GUIANA
Cayenne

Mount Roraima 2810
Guiana Highlands
R. Essequibo
R. Branco
Boa Vista
Pico da Neblina 3014

COLOMBIA
Bogotá
Medellín
Cali
Bucaramanga
Cúcuta
Tunja
Villavicencio
Florencia
Manizales
Barbosa
Cristóbal
San Cristóbal
R. Magdalena
Cordillera Oriental
Cordillera Central
Cordillera Occidental

ECUADOR
Quito
Cotopaxi 5896
Cotopaxi
Ambato
Guayaquil
Machala
Portoviejo
Posto

Equator

PERU
Lima
Trujillo
Chiclayo
Chimbote
Piura
Huancayo
Huascarán 6768
Huánuco
Ayacucho
Arequipa
Pucallpa
Cruzeiro do Sul
Cusco
Juliaca
Puno
Lake Titicaca
Coropuna 6425
Iquique
Arica

Cordillera Occidental
Cordillera Oriental
Cordillera Central
Cord. Occidental

ANDES

BOLIVIA
La Paz
Sucre
Potosí 6542
Cochabamba
Santa Cruz
Trinidad
Oruro
Altiplano

R. Napo
R. Marañón
R. Ucayali
R. Huallaga
R. Putumayo
R. Caquetá
R. Yavarí
R. Juruá
R. Purus
R. Madre de Dios
R. Beni
R. Mamoré
R. Guaporé
R. San Miguel
R. Japurá
R. Negro

Amazon Basin
Manaus
Manacapuru
Balbina Resr.
R. Amazon
R. Solimões
Rio Branco
Porto Velho
Ariquemes
Rondônia

Selvas

B R A Z I L

Mouths of the Amazon
Belém
Ilha de Marajó
Macapá
Altamira
Itaituba
Marabá
Tucuruí Resr.
R. Xingu
R. Iriri
R. Tapajós
R. Teles Pires
R. Jurena
R. Juruena
R. Jiparaná
R. Theodore Roosevelt
R. Madeira
R. Aripuanã

São Luís
Bragança
Parnaíba
Sobral
Fortaleza
Natal
Recife
Caruaru
Maceió
Garanhuns
Aracaju
Salvador
Itabuna
Teresina
Imperatriz
Bacabal
Araguaína
R. Araguaia
R. Tocantins
Petrolina
R. São Francisco
Sobradinho Dam
Paulo Afonso
Feira de Santana
Montes Claros
Serra da Mesa Resr.
Serra do Mesa
Luziânia
Anápolis
Goiânia
Brasília
Planalto do Mato Grosso
Cuiabá
Cáceres
Corumbá
Rondonópolis
Rio Verde
R. Paraguai
R. Taquari
Campo Grande
R. Paraná
Uberlândia
Uberaba
Ituiutaba
Teófilo Otôni
Governador Valadares
Linhares
Vitória
Belo Horizonte
Vitória da Conquista
2033
Itambé

Brazilian Highlands

Equator
10° N
10° S

80° W
70° W
60° W

0 200 400 600 800 1000 1200 km

Scale : One centimetre on this map is the same as 200 kilometres on the ground.

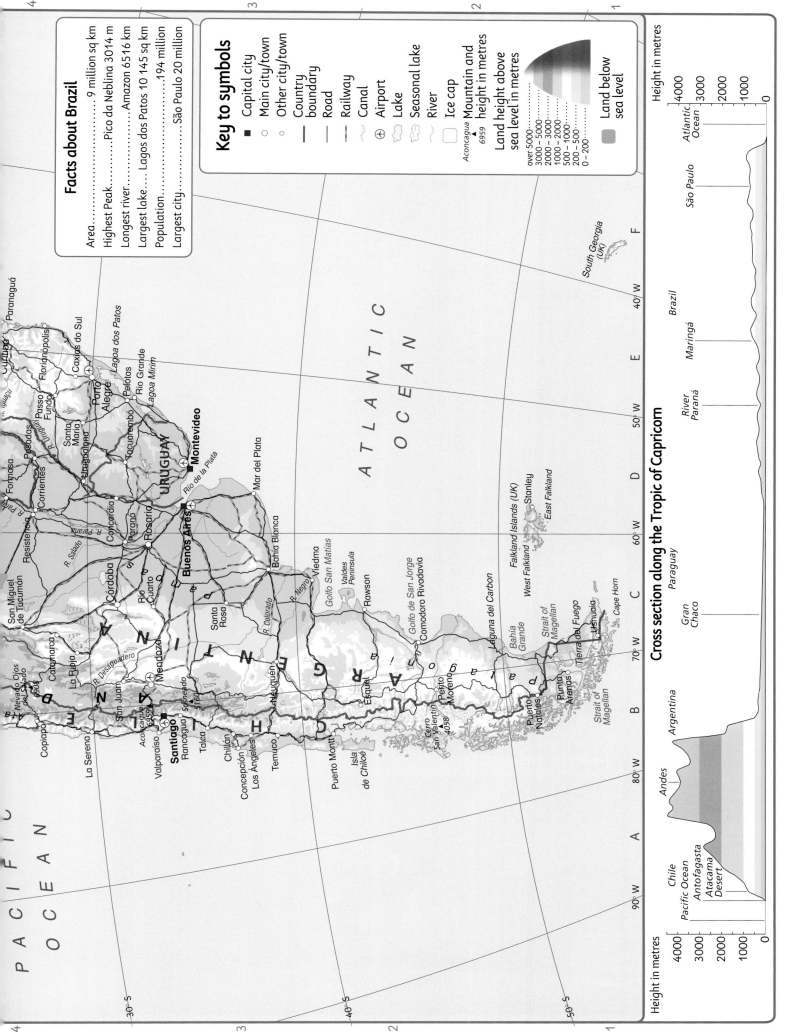

Facts about Brazil

Area...............9 million sq km
Highest Peak......Pico da Neblina 3014 m
Longest river.......Amazon 6516 km
Largest lake....Lagos dos Patos 10 145 sq km
Population...........194 million
Largest city.......São Paulo 20 million

Key to symbols

■ Capital city
○ Main city/town
○ Other city/town
Country boundary
Road
Railway
Canal
⊕ Airport
Lake
Seasonal lake
River
Ice cap
Aconcagua Mountain and height in metres
▲ 6959

Land height above sea level in metres

over 5000
3000 – 5000
2000 – 3000
1000 – 2000
500 – 1000
200 – 500
0 – 200

Land below sea level

Height in metres

4000
3000
2000
1000
0

Cross section along the Tropic of Capricorn

Chile — Pacific Ocean — Antofagasta — Atacama Desert — Andes — Argentina — Gran Chaco — Paraguay — River Paraná — Maringá — Brazil — São Paulo — Atlantic Ocean

Height in metres

4000
3000
2000
1000
0

Australia, New Zealand and Papua New Guinea are the largest countries in Oceania. Other countries are made up of groups of islands scattered across the Pacific Ocean.

Key to symbols
- Countries
- ■ Capital city
- ○ Important city/town

ASIA

New Guinea

PAPUA NEW GUINEA

Lae

■ Port Moresby

Arafura Sea

Timor Sea

Darwin

INDIAN OCEAN

Coral Sea

Cairns

Townsville

SOLOMON ISLANDS

■ Honiara

■ Yaren NAURU

KIRIBA

TUVA

VANUATU

■ Port Vila

New Caledonia (Fr.)

■ Nouméa

FIJI

Rockhampton

Alice Springs

AUSTRALIA

Kalgoorlie

Lake Eyre

Great Australian Bight

Perth

Adelaide

Brisbane

Gold Coast

Largest country
Australia 8 million sq km

PACIFIC OCEAN

Newcastle

Sydney

Country with most people
Australia 21 million

Canberra

Melbourne

Geelong

Tasman Sea

North Island

Auckland

Tasmania

Hobart

NEW ZEALAND

■ Wellington

Total population of Oceania
35 million

Largest city
Sydney 4 million

Christchurch

South Island

Dunedin

Tuvalu is made up of a chain of nine small islands and coral reefs. There are only 12 000 people in the whole country.

Scale : One centimetre on this map is the same as 325 kilometres on the ground.

0 300 600 900 1200 1500 1800 2100 km

Key to symbols

Land height above sea level in metres

- over 5000
- 2000 – 5000
- 1000 – 2000
- 500 – 1000
- 200 – 500
- 0 – 200

Puncak Jaya 5030 ▲ Mountain and height in metres

∼ River

Lake

Seasonal lake

Land below sea level

Oceania has many landscapes. Australia has many deserts, New Zealand and Papua New Guinea have high mountains and there are groups of coral islands in the Pacific Ocean.

Highest mountain
Puncak Jaya 5030 m

Total area of Oceania
9 million sq km

Largest island
New Guinea 808 510 sq km

Largest lake
Lake Eyre 8900 sq km
In dry weather Lake Eyre can dry up completely

Lowest point
Lake Eyre
16 metres below sea level

Longest river
Murray-Darling 3672 km

Puncak Jaya 5030

Mount Wilhelm 4509 ▲

New Guinea

New Ireland

New Britain

Solomon Islands

Arafura Sea

Timor Sea

Arnhem Land

Gulf of Carpentaria

Cape York Peninsula

Great Barrier Reef

Coral Sea

INDIAN OCEAN

Kimberley Plateau

R. Fitzroy

Great Sandy Desert

Macdonnell Ranges

R. Fortescue

Australia

867 ▲ Uluru (Ayers Rock)

Musgrave Ranges

Great Victoria Desert

Lake Eyre

Lake Torrens

Nullarbor Plain

Great Australian Bight

Cape Leeuwin

R. Murray

R. Darling

R. Macquarie

R. Lachlan

R. Murrumbidgee

R. Murray

Mount Kosciuszko 2229 ▲

Great Dividing Range

Fiji

New Caledonia

PACIFIC OCEAN

Tasman Sea

Tasmania

North Cape

North Island

New Zealand

Aoraki (Mount Cook) 3754 ▲

South Island

Aoraki (Mount Cook) is the highest mountain in New Zealand. The name means 'cloud piercer' in the local language.

Uluṟu (Ayers Rock) in the middle of Australia is a World Heritage site and a holy place for Aborigines.

300 600 900 1200 1500 1800 2100 km

Scale : One centimetre on this map is the same as 325 kilometres on the ground.

The Arctic Ocean is the smallest of the world's oceans. It is very cold and mostly covered with sea ice. In summer whales, seals and other creatures come to the Arctic Ocean looking for food.

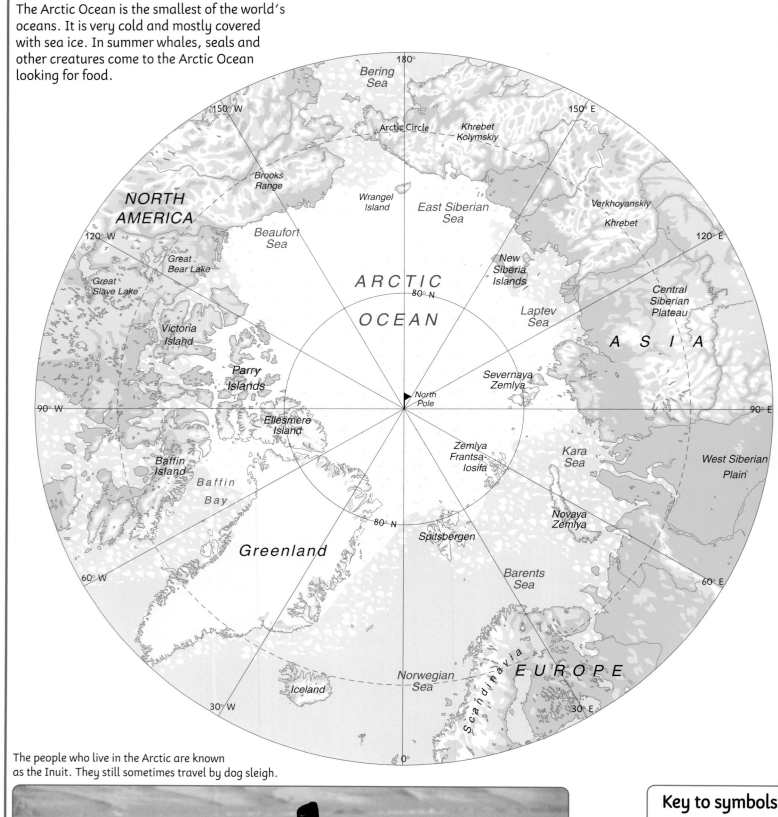

180°

Bering Sea

150° W

Arctic Circle

Khrebet Kolymskiy

150° E

Brooks Range

Wrangel Island

East Siberian Sea

Verkhoyanskiy Khrebet

NORTH AMERICA

120° W

Beaufort Sea

New Siberia Islands

120° E

Great Bear Lake

Central Siberian Plateau

Great Slave Lake

A R C T I C

Laptev Sea

80° N

A S I A

Victoria Island

O C E A N

Severnaya Zemlya

Parry Islands

90° W

Ellesmere Island

North Pole

90° E

Zemlya Frantsa-Iosifa

Kara Sea

West Siberian Plain

Baffin Island

Baffin Bay

80° N

Novaya Zemlya

Spitsbergen

Greenland

Barents Sea

60° W

60° E

Norwegian Sea

Scandinavia

E U R O P E

30° W

Iceland

30° E

0°

The people who live in the Arctic are known as the Inuit. They still sometimes travel by dog sleigh.

Key to symbols

Land height above sea level in metres

over 2000
1000 – 2000
500 – 1000
200 – 500
0 – 200

River

Lake

Ice cap

Polar pack ice

Drifting ice

0   500   1000   1500   2000 km

Scale : One centimetre on this map is the same as 350 kilometres on the ground.

Names of bases numbered on map
1 Comandante Ferraz (Brazil)
2 King Sejong (South Korea)
3 Artigas (Uruguay)
4 Frei (Chile)
5 Bellingshausen (Russian Federation)
6 Great Wall (China)
7 Escudero (Chile)
8 Jubany (Argentina)
9 Arctowski (Poland)
10 O'Higgins (Chile)
11 San Martin (Argentina)

Antarctica is the world's coldest, driest and windiest continent. It is covered by a thick sheet of ice. In many places the ice is thicker than the highest mountains in the UK. Very few plants and animals survive here.

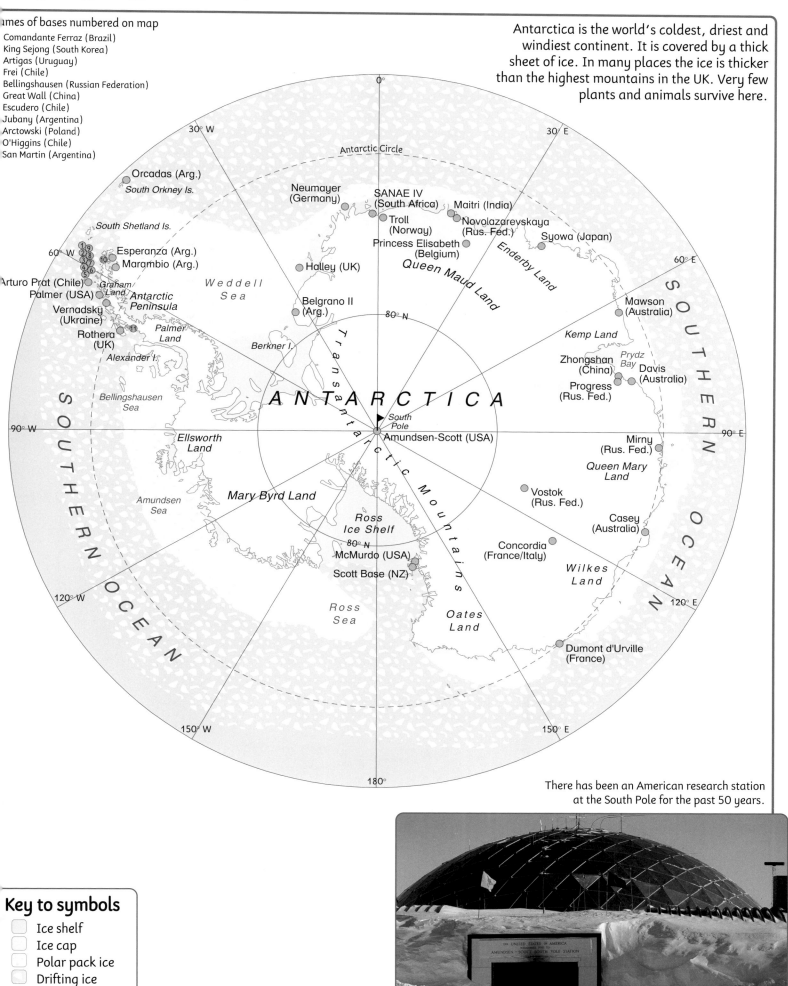

There has been an American research station at the South Pole for the past 50 years.

Key to symbols
Ice shelf
Ice cap
Polar pack ice
Drifting ice
● Manned bases

500 1000 1500 2000 km

Scale : One centimetre on this map is the same as 350 kilometres on the ground.

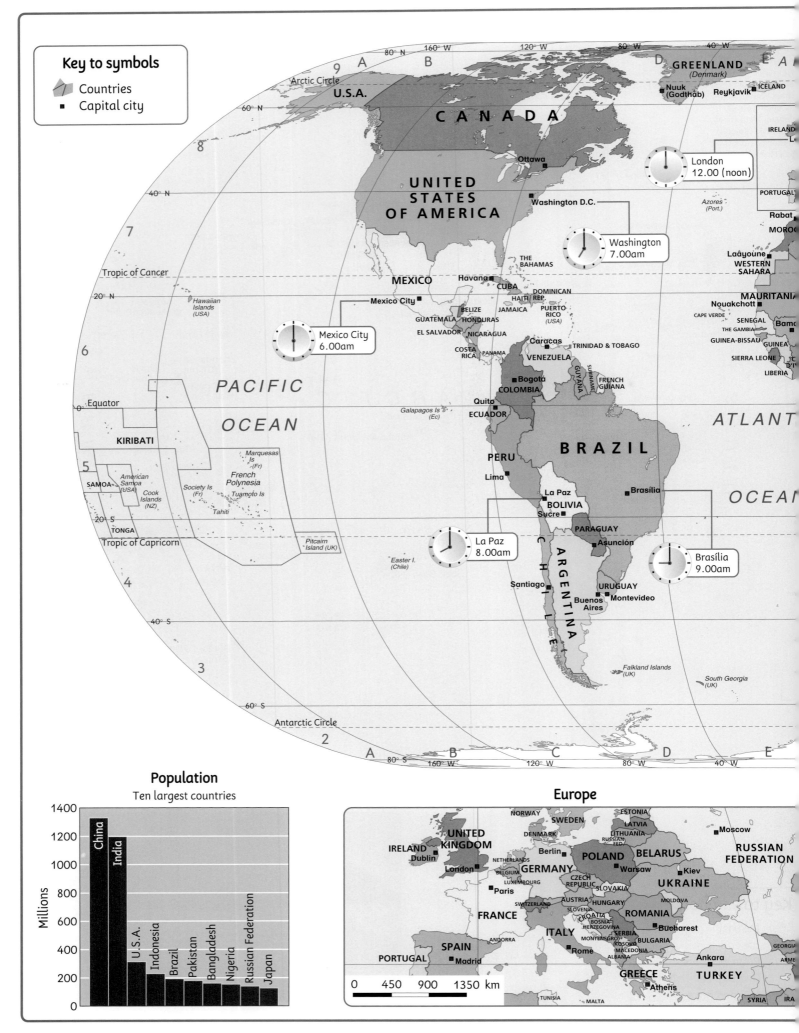

Key to symbols

Countries

■ Capital city

London 12.00 (noon)

Washington 7.00am

Mexico City 6.00am

La Paz 8.00am

Brasília 9.00am

GREENLAND (Denmark)

Nuuk (Godthåb)   Reykjavik   ICELAND

Arctic Circle

U.S.A.

C A N A D A

IRELAND

Ottawa

UNITED STATES OF AMERICA

Washington D.C.

PORTUGAL

Azores (Port.)

Rabat

MOROC

Laâyoune
WESTERN SAHARA

Tropic of Cancer

MEXICO   Havana
CUBA
THE BAHAMAS

MAURITANIA

Nouakchott

Mexico City

HAITI   DOMINICAN REP.
BELIZE   JAMAICA   PUERTO RICO (USA)
GUATEMALA   HONDURAS
EL SALVADOR   NICARAGUA
COSTA RICA   PANAMA

Hawaiian Islands (USA)

CAPE VERDE   SENEGAL
THE GAMBIA   Bamo
GUINEA-BISSAU   GUINEA
SIERRA LEONE   D'I
LIBERIA

Caracas   TRINIDAD & TOBAGO
VENEZUELA

Bogotá
COLOMBIA   GUYANA   SURINAME   FRENCH GUIANA

Quito
ECUADOR

Galapagos Is (Ec)

PACIFIC

Equator

OCEAN

ATLANT

KIRIBATI

B R A Z I L

Marquesas Is (Fr)

PERU

French Polynesia

Society Is (Fr)
Tuamoto Is

Lima

OCEAN

SAMOA   American Samoa (USA)   Cook Islands (NZ)

La Paz
BOLIVIA
Sucre

Brasília

Tahiti

PARAGUAY

TONGA

Tropic of Capricorn

Pitcairn Island (UK)

Easter I. (Chile)

Asunción

A R G E N T I N A

C H I L E

URUGUAY

Santiago   Buenos Aires   Montevideo

Falkland Islands (UK)

South Georgia (UK)

Antarctic Circle

Population
Ten largest countries

China
India
U.S.A.
Indonesia
Brazil
Pakistan
Bangladesh
Nigeria
Russian Federation
Japan

Millions

1400
1200
1000
800
600
400
200
0

Europe

NORWAY   SWEDEN   ESTONIA   LATVIA   LITHUANIA   Moscow
DENMARK   RUSSIAN FED.
UNITED KINGDOM   Berlin   POLAND   BELARUS   RUSSIAN FEDERATION
IRELAND   Dublin   NETHERLANDS   GERMANY   Warsaw   Kiev
London   BELGIUM   LUXEMBOURG   UKRAINE
Paris   CZECH REPUBLIC   SLOVAKIA
SWITZERLAND   AUSTRIA   HUNGARY   MOLDOVA
FRANCE   SLOVENIA   ROMANIA   GEORGIA
CROATIA   BOSNIA-HERZEGOVINA   SERBIA   Bucharest
ANDORRA   ITALY   MONTENEGRO   KOSOVO   BULGARIA   ARME
SPAIN   Rome   MACEDONIA   Ankara
PORTUGAL   Madrid   ALBANIA   TURKEY
GREECE
TUNISIA   MALTA   Athens   SYRIA   IRA

0   450   900   1350 km

0   850   1700   2550   3400 km

Scale : One centimetre on this map is the same as 850 kilometres on the ground.

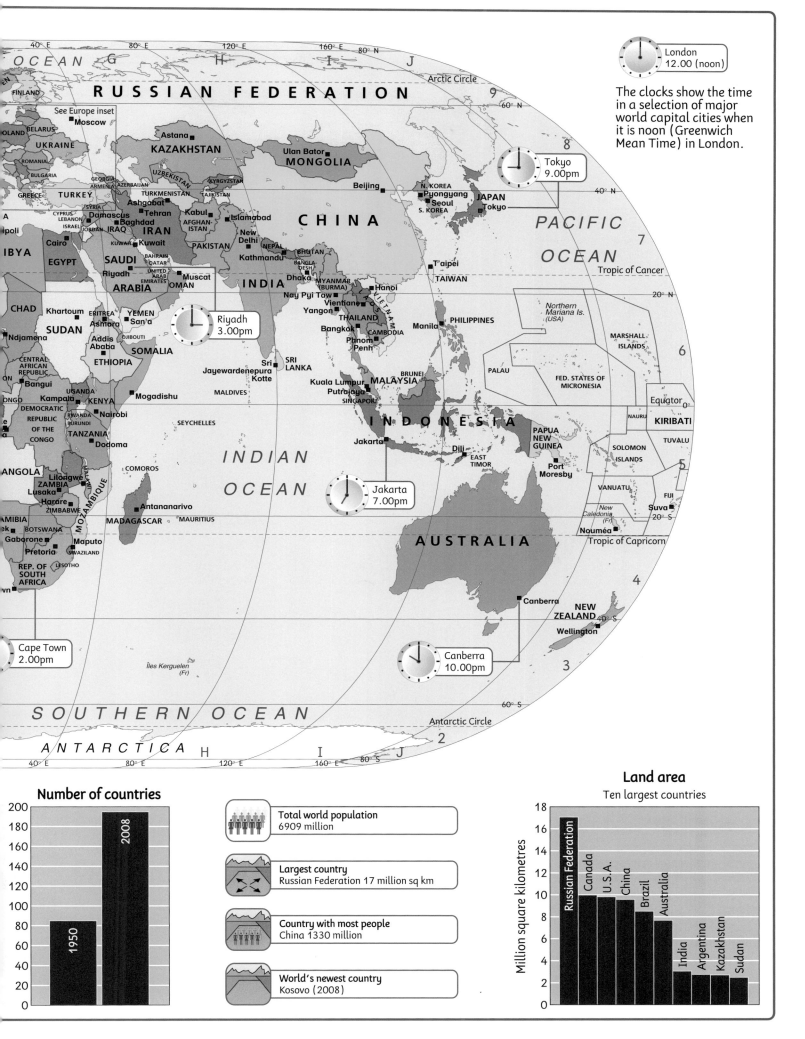

The clocks show the time in a selection of major world capital cities when it is noon (Greenwich Mean Time) in London.

London 12.00 (noon)

Tokyo 9.00pm

Riyadh 3.00pm

Jakarta 7.00pm

Canberra 10.00pm

Cape Town 2.00pm

Number of countries

1950
2008

Land area
Ten largest countries

Million square kilometres

Russian Federation
Canada
U.S.A.
China
Brazil
Australia
India
Argentina
Kazakhstan
Sudan

Total world population 6909 million

Largest country Russian Federation 17 million sq km

Country with most people China 1330 million

World's newest country Kosovo (2008)

Asia is the world's largest continent.

ASIA

Total area
509 million sq km

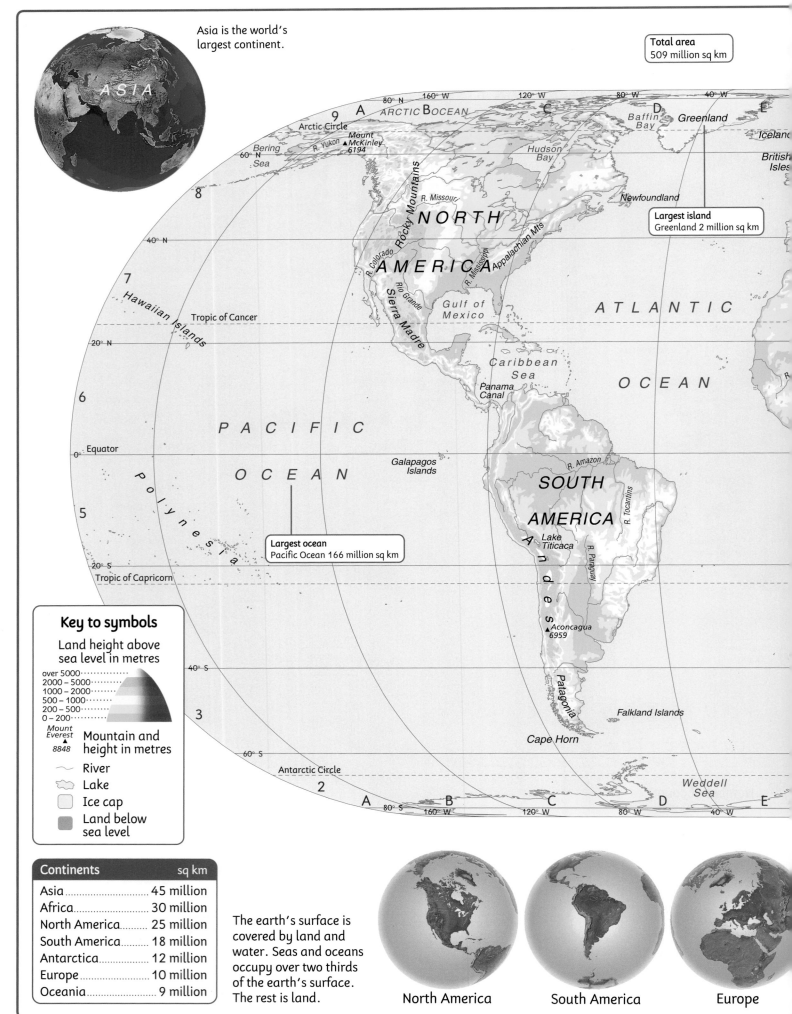

Arctic Circle

Bering Sea

60° N

Mount McKinley 6194

R. Yukon

80° N

ARCTIC OCEAN

160° W

120° W

80° W

40° W

Baffin Bay

Greenland

Iceland

British Isles

Hudson Bay

Newfoundland

Largest island
Greenland 2 million sq km

Rocky Mountains

R. Missouri

NORTH

40° N

R. Colorado

AMERICA

R. Mississippi

Appalachian Mts

7

Sierra Madre

Rio Grande

Gulf of Mexico

ATLANTIC

Hawaiian Islands

Tropic of Cancer

20° N

Caribbean Sea

OCEAN

6

Panama Canal

PACIFIC

Equator

0°

OCEAN

Galapagos Islands

R. Amazon

SOUTH

Polynesia

5

AMERICA

R. Tocantins

Largest ocean
Pacific Ocean 166 million sq km

Andes

Lake Titicaca

R. Paraguay

20° S

Tropic of Capricorn

Key to symbols

Land height above
sea level in metres

over 5000
2000 – 5000
1000 – 2000
500 – 1000
200 – 500
0 – 200

40° S

Aconcagua
6959

Mount Everest
8848

▲ Mountain and
height in metres

Patagonia

Falkland Islands

~ River

3

Lake

Cape Horn

Ice cap

60° S

Antarctic Circle

Land below
sea level

2

Weddell Sea

A

80° S

B

160° W

C

120° W

D

80° W

E

40° W

Continents	sq km
Asia	45 million
Africa	30 million
North America	25 million
South America	18 million
Antarctica	12 million
Europe	10 million
Oceania	9 million

The earth's surface is
covered by land and
water. Seas and oceans
occupy over two thirds
of the earth's surface.
The rest is land.

North America   South America   Europe

Scale : One centimetre on this map is the same as 850 kilometres on the ground.

The Pacific Ocean covers nearly half of the Earth.

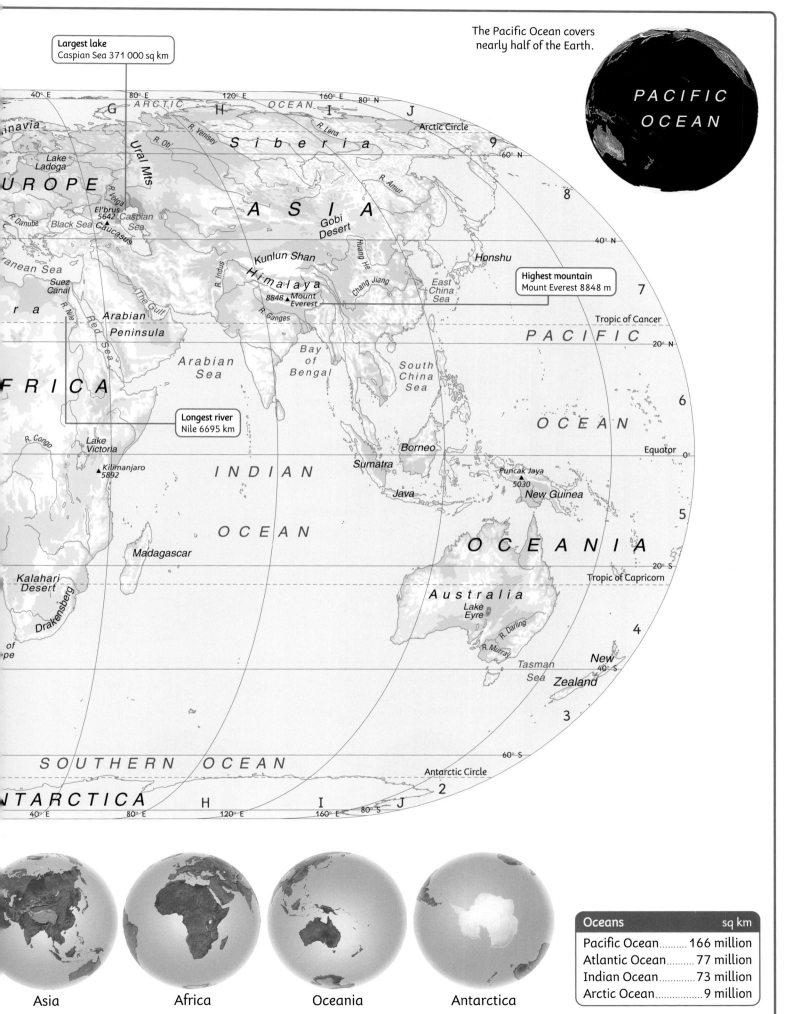

Largest lake
Caspian Sea 371 000 sq km

Highest mountain
Mount Everest 8848 m

Longest river
Nile 6695 km

PACIFIC OCEAN

ARCTIC OCEAN
Arctic Circle
60° N
Siberia
R. Yenisey
R. Lena
80° N
9
8
R. Ob'
ASIA
R. Amur
40° N
EUROPE
Lake Ladoga
Ural Mts
R. Volga
El'brus 5642
Caspian Sea
Caucasus
Gobi Desert
Honshu
R. Danube
Black Sea
Kunlun Shan
Huang He
Himalaya
Chang Jiang
East China Sea
7
Mediterranean Sea
Suez Canal
The Gulf
R. Indus
8848 Mount Everest
Tropic of Cancer
20° N
Sahara
R. Nile
Arabian Peninsula
R. Ganges
PACIFIC
Red Sea
Arabian Sea
Bay of Bengal
South China Sea
OCEAN
6
AFRICA
R. Congo
Lake Victoria
Borneo
Equator
0°
Kilimanjaro 5892
INDIAN
Sumatra
Puncak Jaya 5030
New Guinea
5
Java
OCEAN
Madagascar
OCEANIA
20° S
Kalahari Desert
Tropic of Capricorn
Drakensberg
Australia
Lake Eyre
R. Darling
4
Cape of Good Hope
R. Murray
New Zealand
Tasman Sea
40° S
3
SOUTHERN OCEAN
60° S
Antarctic Circle
2
ANTARCTICA
40° E
80° E
120° E
160° E
80° S

Asia

Africa

Oceania

Antarctica

Oceans	sq km
Pacific Ocean	166 million
Atlantic Ocean	77 million
Indian Ocean	73 million
Arctic Ocean	9 million

Climate graphs

The red line shows average temperature.
The blue bars show average monthly rainfall.

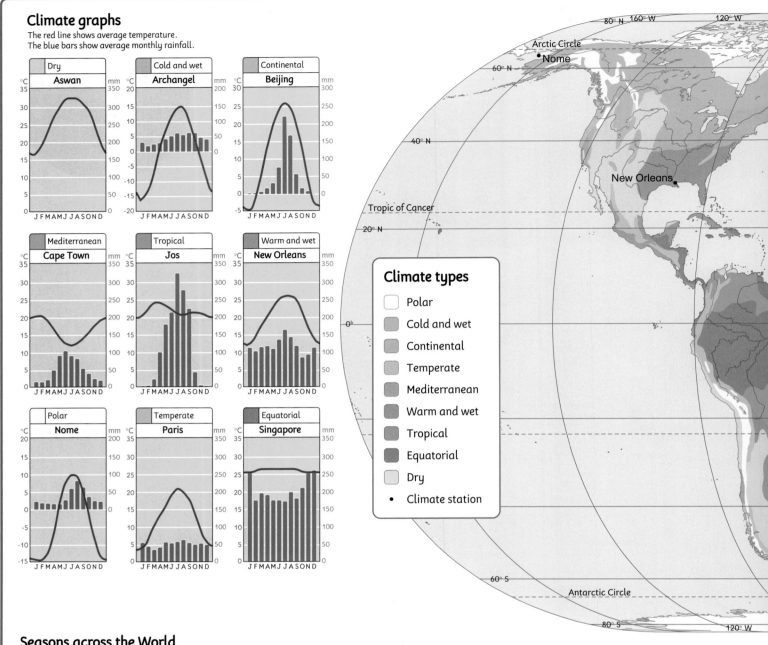

Seasons across the World

The year is divided into seasons. The length of each season can vary depending on how far a place is from the equator. These dials show the pattern of seasons in the northern hemisphere.

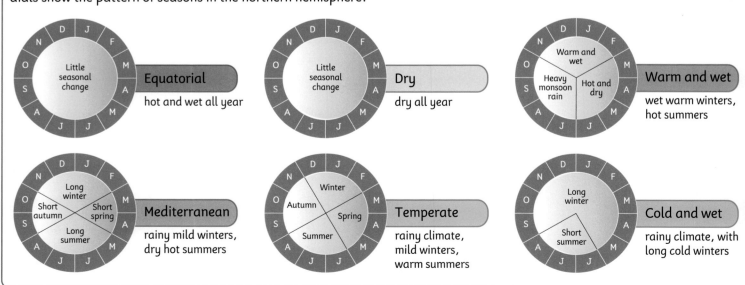

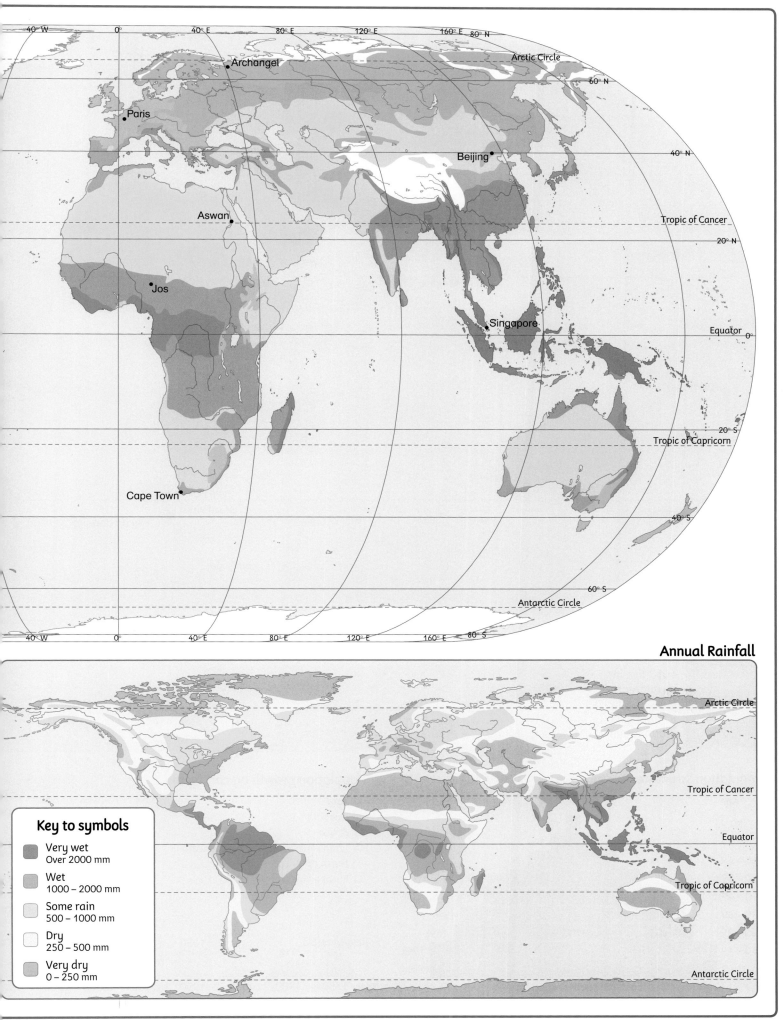

Annual Rainfall

Key to symbols

- **Very wet**
  Over 2000 mm
- **Wet**
  1000 – 2000 mm
- **Some rain**
  500 – 1000 mm
- **Dry**
  250 – 500 mm
- **Very dry**
  0 – 250 mm

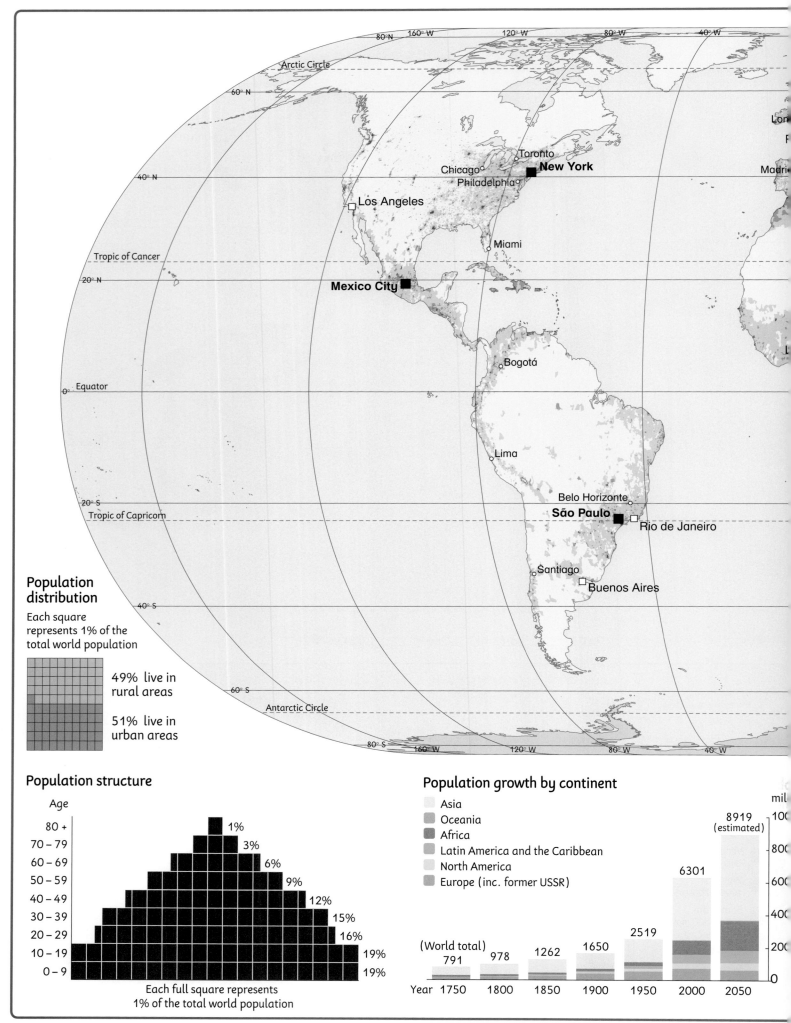

Population distribution

Each square represents 1% of the total world population

49% live in rural areas

51% live in urban areas

Population structure

Age

80 +	1%
70 – 79	3%
60 – 69	6%
50 – 59	9%
40 – 49	12%
30 – 39	15%
20 – 29	16%
10 – 19	19%
0 – 9	19%

Each full square represents 1% of the total world population

Population growth by continent

mil

Asia
Oceania
Africa
Latin America and the Caribbean
North America
Europe (inc. former USSR)

(World total)

Year	1750	1800	1850	1900	1950	2000	2050
	791	978	1262	1650	2519	6301	8919 (estimated)

Scale : One centimetre on this map is the same as 850 kilometres on the ground.

0 1000 2000 3000 4000 km

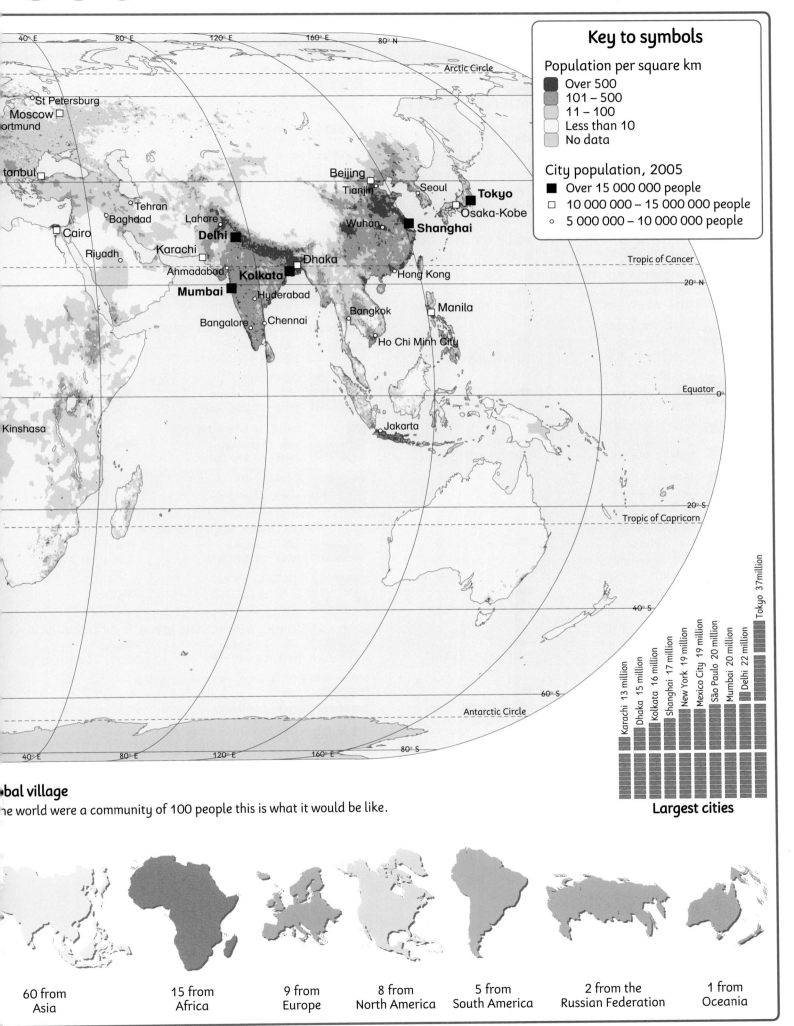

Key to symbols

Population per square km
- Over 500
- 101 – 500
- 11 – 100
- Less than 10
- No data

City population, 2005
- ■ Over 15 000 000 people
- □ 10 000 000 – 15 000 000 people
- ○ 5 000 000 – 10 000 000 people

Arctic Circle

St Petersburg
Moscow
Dortmund
Istanbul
Tehran
Baghdad
Lahore
Cairo
Riyadh
Karachi
Ahmadabad
Delhi
Kolkata
Mumbai
Hyderabad
Bangalore
Chennai
Dhaka
Beijing
Tianjin
Wuhan
Seoul
Tokyo
Osaka-Kobe
Shanghai
Hong Kong
Bangkok
Manila
Ho Chi Minh City
Jakarta
Kinshasa

Tropic of Cancer

20° N

Equator   0°

20° S

Tropic of Capricorn

40° S

60° S

Antarctic Circle

Largest cities

Karachi 13 million
Dhaka 15 million
Kolkata 16 million
Shanghai 17 million
New York 19 million
Mexico City 19 million
São Paulo 20 million
Mumbai 20 million
Delhi 22 million
Tokyo 37million

Global village

If the world were a community of 100 people this is what it would be like.

| 60 from Asia | 15 from Africa | 9 from Europe | 8 from North America | 5 from South America | 2 from the Russian Federation | 1 from Oceania |

Flag	COUNTRY, CONTINENT / Capital City / Population	Ecological footprint* / Area (square km)

	AFGHANISTAN, ASIA	
	Kabul	n/a
	28 150 000	652 225 sq km

	ALBANIA, EUROPE	
	Tiranë	2.6
	3 155 000	28 748 sq km

	ALGERIA, AFRICA	
	Algiers	1.9
	34 895 000	2 381 741 sq km

	ANGOLA, AFRICA	
	Luanda	0.9
	18 498 000	1 246 700 sq km

	ARGENTINA, SOUTH AMERICA	
	Buenos Aires	3
	40 276 000	2 766 889 sq km

	ARMENIA, ASIA	
	Yerevan	1.6
	3 083 000	29 800 sq km

	AUSTRALIA, OCEANIA	
	Canberra	n/a
	21 293 000	7 692 024 sq km

	AUSTRIA, EUROPE	
	Vienna	4.9
	8 364 000	83 855 sq km

	BAHRAIN, ASIA	
	Manama	n/a
	791 000	691 sq km

	BANGLADESH, ASIA	
	Dhaka	n/a
	162 221 000	143 998 sq km

	BELARUS, EUROPE	
	Minsk	4.2
	9 634 000	207 600 sq km

	BELGIUM, EUROPE	
	Brussels	5.7
	10 647 000	30 520 sq km

	BENIN, AFRICA	
	Porto Novo	1
	8 935 000	112 620 sq km

	BHUTAN, ASIA	
	Thimphu	n/a
	697 000	46 620 sq km

	BOLIVIA, SOUTH AMERICA	
	La Paz/Sucre	2.4
	9 863 000	1 098 581 sq km

	BOSNIA-HERZEGOVINA, EUROPE	
	Sarajevo	3.4
	3 767 000	51 130 sq km

	BOTSWANA, AFRICA	
	Gaborone	3.9
	1 950 000	581 370 sq km

	BRAZIL, SOUTH AMERICA	
	Brasília	n/a
	193 734 000	8 514 879 sq km

	BRUNEI, ASIA	
	Bandar Seri Begawan	n/a
	400 000	5 765 sq km

	BULGARIA, EUROPE	
	Sofia	3.3
	7 545 000	110 994 sq km

	BURKINA FASO, AFRICA	
	Ouagadougou	1.4
	15 757 000	274 200 sq km

	BURUNDI, AFRICA	
	Bujumbura	n/a
	8 303 000	27 835 sq km

	CAMBODIA, ASIA	
	Phnom Penh	0.9
	14 805 000	181 035 sq km

	CAMEROON, AFRICA	
	Yaoundé	1.1
	19 522 000	475 442 sq km

	CANADA, NORTH AMERICA	
	Ottawa	5.8
	33 573 000	9 984 670 sq km

	CENTRAL AFRICAN REPUBLIC, AFRICA	
	Bangui	1.4
	4 422 000	622 436 sq km

	CHAD, AFRICA	
	Ndjamena	1.8
	11 206 000	1 284 000 sq km

	CHILE, SOUTH AMERICA	
	Santiago	3.1
	16 970 000	756 945 sq km

	CHINA, ASIA	
	Beijing	1.8
	1 330 265 000	9 584 492 sq km

	COLOMBIA, SOUTH AMERICA	
	Bogotá	1.9
	45 660 000	1 141 748 sq km

	CONGO, AFRICA	
	Brazzaville	1
	3 683 000	342 000 sq km

	CONGO, DEMOCRATIC REPUBLIC OF THE, AFRICA	
	Kinshasa	0.7
	66 020 000	2 345 410 sq km

	COSTA RICA, NORTH AMERICA	
	San José	2.7
	4 579 000	51 100 sq km

	CÔTE D'IVOIRE, AFRICA	
	Yamoussoukro	0.9
	21 075 000	322 463 sq km

	CROATIA, EUROPE	
	Zagreb	3.3
	4 416 000	56 538 sq km

	CUBA, NORTH AMERICA	
	Havana	2.3
	11 204 000	110 860 sq km

	CYPRUS, ASIA	
	Nicosia	n/a
	871 000	9 251 sq km

	CZECH REPUBLIC, EUROPE	
	Prague	5.3
	10 369 000	78 864 sq km

	DENMARK, EUROPE	
	Copenhagen	7.2
	5 470 000	43 075 sq km

*(global hectares per capita). Ecological footprints are a way of comparing consumption, lifestyle and environmental sustainability. High figures indicate high consumption, while low figures indicate greater sustainability. The world average is 1.8 gha per capita.

DJIBOUTI, AFRICA
Djibouti
864 000
0.9
23 200 sq km

DOMINICAN REPUBLIC, NORTH AMERICA
Santo Domingo
10 090 000
1.4
48 442 sq km

EAST TIMOR, ASIA
Dili
1 134 000
n/a
14 874 sq km

ECUADOR, SOUTH AMERICA
Quito
13 625 000
1.9
272 045 sq km

EGYPT, AFRICA
Cairo
82 999 000
1.4
1 001 450 sq km

EL SALVADOR, NORTH AMERICA
San Salvador
6 163 000
n/a
21 041 sq km

ERITREA, AFRICA
Asmara
5 073 000
0.8
117 400 sq km

ESTONIA, EUROPE
Tallinn
1 340 000
6.4
45 200 sq km

ETHIOPIA, AFRICA
Addis Ababa
82 825 000
n/a
1 133 880 sq km

FINLAND, EUROPE
Helsinki
5 326 000
5.5
338 145 sq km

FRANCE, EUROPE
Paris
62 343 000
4.6
543 965 sq km

GABON, AFRICA
Libreville
1 475 000
n/a
267 667 sq km

GEORGIA, ASIA
T'bilisi
4 260 000
n/a
69 700 sq km

GERMANY, EUROPE
Berlin
82 167 000
4
357 022 sq km

GHANA, AFRICA
Accra
23 837 000
1.6
238 537 sq km

GREECE, EUROPE
Athens
11 161 000
5.8
131 957 sq km

GUATEMALA, NORTH AMERICA
Guatemala City
14 027 000
1.7
108 890 sq km

GUINEA, AFRICA
Conakry
10 069 000
1.5
245 857 sq km

GUINEA-BISSAU, AFRICA
Bissau
1 611 000
1
36 125 sq km

GUYANA, SOUTH AMERICA
Georgetown
762 000
n/a
214 969 sq km

HAITI, NORTH AMERICA
Port-au-Prince
10 033 000
0.5
27 750 sq km

HONDURAS, NORTH AMERICA
Tegucigalpa
7 466 000
2.2
112 088 sq km

HUNGARY, EUROPE
Budapest
9 993 000
3.2
93 030 sq km

ICELAND, EUROPE
Reykjavik
323 000
n/a
102 820 sq km

INDIA, ASIA
New Delhi
1 198 003 000
0.8
3 064 898 sq km

INDONESIA, ASIA
Jakarta
229 965 000
n/a
1 919 445 sq km

IRAN, ASIA
Tehran
74 196 000
2.7
1 648 000 sq km

IRAQ, ASIA
Baghdad
30 747 000
1.3
438 317 sq km

IRELAND, EUROPE
Dublin
4 515 000
8.2
70 282 sq km

ISRAEL, ASIA
Jerusalem
7 170 000
5.4
20 770 sq km

ITALY, EUROPE
Rome
59 870 000
4.9
301 245 sq km

JAMAICA, NORTH AMERICA
Kingston
2 719 000
n/a
10 991 sq km

JAPAN, ASIA
Tokyo
127 156 000
4.1
377 727 sq km

JORDAN, ASIA
Amman
6 316 000
2
89 206 sq km

KAZAKHSTAN, ASIA
Astana
15 637 000
4.4
2 717 300 sq km

KENYA, AFRICA
Nairobi
39 802 000
n/a
582 646 sq km

KOSOVO, EUROPE
Pristina
2 153 000
n/a
10 908 sq km

KUWAIT, ASIA
Kuwait
2 985 000
7.9
17 818 sq km

KYRGYZSTAN, ASIA
Bishkek
5 482 000
1.3
198 500 sq km

LAOS, ASIA
Vientiane
6 320 000
1
236 800 sq km

LATVIA, EUROPE		
Riga		4.6
2 249 000		64 589 sq km

LEBANON, ASIA		
Beirut		2.1
4 224 000		10 452 sq km

LESOTHO, AFRICA		
Maseru		n/a
2 067 000		30 355 sq km

LIBERIA, AFRICA		
Monrovia		1.2
3 955 000		111 369 sq km

LIBYA, AFRICA		
Tripoli		3.2
6 420 000		1 759 540 sq km

LITHUANIA, EUROPE		
Vilnius		3.3
3 287 000		65 200 sq km

LUXEMBOURG, EUROPE		
Luxembourg		n/a
486 000		2 586 sq km

MACEDONIA (F.Y.R.O.M.), EUROPE		
Skopje		n/a
2 042 000		25 713 sq km

MADAGASCAR, AFRICA		
Antananarivo		1.2
19 625 000		587 041 sq km

MALAWI, AFRICA		
Lilongwe		n/a
15 263 000		118 484 sq km

MALAYSIA, ASIA		
Kuala Lumpur/Putrajaya		n/a
27 468 000		332 965 sq km

MALI, AFRICA		
Bamako		1.9
13 010 000		1 240 140 sq km

MAURITANIA, AFRICA		
Nouakchott		3.1
3 291 000		1 030 700 sq km

MEXICO, NORTH AMERICA		
Mexico City		3.2
109 610 000		1 972 545 sq km

MOLDOVA, EUROPE		
Chișinău		1.7
3 604 000		33 700 sq km

MONGOLIA, ASIA		
Ulan Bator		n/a
2 671 000		1 565 000 sq km

MONTENEGRO, EUROPE		
Podgorica		n/a
624 000		13 812 sq km

MOROCCO, AFRICA		
Rabat		1.3
31 993 000		446 550 sq km

MOZAMBIQUE, AFRICA		
Maputo		n/a
22 894 000		799 380 sq km

MYANMAR (BURMA), ASIA		
Nay Pyi Taw/Yangon		1
50 020 000		676 577 sq km

NAMIBIA, AFRICA		
Windhoek		3
2 171 000		824 292 sq km

NEPAL, ASIA		
Kathmandu		n/a
29 331 000		147 181 sq km

NETHERLANDS, EUROPE		
Amsterdam/The Hague		4.6
16 592 000		41 526 sq km

NEW ZEALAND, OCEANIA		
Wellington		7.6
4 266 000		270 534 sq km

NICARAGUA, NORTH AMERICA		
Managua		2.3
5 743 000		130 000 sq km

NIGER, AFRICA		
Niamey		1.7
15 290 000		1 267 000 sq km

NIGERIA, AFRICA		
Abuja		1.6
154 729 000		923 768 sq km

NORTH KOREA, ASIA		
Pyongyang		1.4
23 906 000		120 538 sq km

NORWAY, EUROPE		
Oslo		4.2
4 812 000		323 878 sq km

OMAN, ASIA		
Muscat		3.5
2 845 000		309 500 sq km

PAKISTAN, ASIA		
Islamabad		0.7
180 808 000		803 940 sq km

PANAMA, NORTH AMERICA		
Panama City		3.2
3 454 000		77 082 sq km

PAPUA NEW GUINEA, OCEANIA		
Port Moresby		1.7
6 732 000		462 840 sq km

PARAGUAY, SOUTH AMERICA		
Asunción		3.4
6 349 000		406 752 sq km

PERU, SOUTH AMERICA		
Lima		1.8
29 165 000		1 285 216 sq km

PHILIPPINES, ASIA		
Manila		n/a
91 983 000		300 000 sq km

POLAND, EUROPE		
Warsaw		3.9
38 074 000		312 683 sq km

PORTUGAL, EUROPE		
Lisbon		4.4
10 707 000		88 940 sq km

QATAR, ASIA		
Doha		9.7
1 409 000		11 437 sq km

ROMANIA, EUROPE		
Bucharest		2.7
21 275 000		237 500 sq km

RUSSIAN FEDERATION, EUROPE/ASIA
Moscow 4.4
140 874 000 17 075 400 sq km

SAUDI ARABIA, ASIA
Riyadh 3.5
25 721 000 2 200 000 sq km

SENEGAL, AFRICA
Dakar 1.2
12 534 000 196 720 sq km

SERBIA, EUROPE
Belgrade n/a
7 335 000 77 453 sq km

SIERRA LEONE, AFRICA
Freetown 0.8
5 696 000 71 740 sq km

SINGAPORE, ASIA
Singapore 4.5
4 737 000 639 sq km

SLOVAKIA, EUROPE
Bratislava 4.9
5 406 000 49 035 sq km

SLOVENIA, EUROPE
Ljubljana 3.9
2 020 000 20 251 sq km

SOMALIA, AFRICA
Mogadishu 1.5
9 133 000 637 657 sq km

SOUTH AFRICA, REPUBLIC OF, AFRICA
Pretoria/Cape Town 2.7
50 110 000 1 219 090 sq km

SOUTH KOREA, ASIA
Seoul 3.7
48 333 000 99 274 sq km

SPAIN, EUROPE
Madrid 5.6
44 904 000 504 782 sq km

SRI LANKA, ASIA
Sri Jayewardenepura Kotte 0.9
20 238 000 65 610 sq km

SUDAN, AFRICA
Khartoum 2.2
42 272 000 2 505 813 sq km

SURINAME, SOUTH AMERICA
Paramaribo n/a
520 000 163 820 sq km

SWAZILAND, AFRICA
Mbabane n/a
1 185 000 17 364 sq km

SWEDEN, EUROPE
Stockholm n/a
9 249 000 449 964 sq km

SWITZERLAND, EUROPE
Bern 5.6
7 568 000 41 293 sq km

SYRIA, ASIA
Damascus 1.6
21 906 000 185 180 sq km

TAJIKISTAN, ASIA
Dushanbe 0.9
6 952 000 143 100 sq km

TANZANIA, AFRICA
Dodoma 1
43 479 000 945 087 sq km

THAILAND, ASIA
Bangkok 1.7
67 764 000 513 115 sq km

THE GAMBIA, AFRICA
Banjul 1.1
1 705 000 11 295 sq km

TOGO, AFRICA
Lomé n/a
6 619 000 56 785 sq km

TRINIDAD AND TOBAGO, SOUTH AMERICA
Port of Spain n/a
1 339 000 5 130 sq km

TUNISIA, AFRICA
Tunis 1.9
10 272 000 164 150 sq km

TURKEY, ASIA/EUROPE
Ankara 2.8
74 816 000 779 452 sq km

TURKMENISTAN, ASIA
Ashgabat 3.8
5 110 000 488 100 sq km

UGANDA, AFRICA
Kampala n/a
32 710 000 241 038 sq km

UKRAINE, EUROPE
Kiev 2.7
45 708 000 603 700 sq km

UNITED ARAB EMIRATES, ASIA
Abu Dhabi 10.3
4 599 000 77 700 sq km

UNITED KINGDOM, EUROPE
London n/a
61 565 000 243 609 sq km

UNITED STATES OF AMERICA, NORTH AMERICA
Washington 9
314 659 000 9 826 635 sq km

URUGUAY, SOUTH AMERICA
Montevideo n/a
3 361 000 176 215 sq km

UZBEKISTAN, ASIA
Tashkent 1.7
27 488 000 447 400 sq km

VENEZUELA, SOUTH AMERICA
Caracas 2.3
28 583 000 912 050 sq km

VIETNAM, ASIA
Hanoi 1
88 069 000 329 565 sq km

YEMEN, ASIA
San'a 1
23 580 000 527 968 sq km

ZAMBIA, AFRICA
Lusaka 1.2
12 935 000 752 614 sq km

ZIMBABWE, AFRICA
Harare 1
12 523 000 390 759 sq km

place name	grid code	place name	grid code	place name	grid code	place name	grid code
Nairobi *capital* **35 C4**		**Severn** *river* **16 E3**		**Switzerland** *country* **30 F4**		**Borneo** *island* **41 D3**	
page number		page number		page number		page number	
cities and towns are shown in green		water features are shown in blue		countries and states are shown in red		physical features are shown in black	

Photo credits

Corbis:
P 9 Houses of Parliament, London Aerial Photo Library; p 10 Drilling Rig, Bob Fleumer/zefa; p 11 Snow covered mountain, James Murdoch, Cordaiy Photo Library; p 12 Stormont, Geray Sweeney; p 14 Derwent Water, Steven Vidler/Eurasia Press; p 16 Wind Farm, Phil Noble/Reuters; p 17 Eden Project, Ashley Cooper; p 19 London skyline, Ethel Davies/Robert Harding World Imagery; p 20 Hound Tor, Bryan Pickering, Eye Ubiquitous; Applecross, Ric Ergenbright; p 22 Tewkesbury flood, Lee Sanders/epa; p 25 European Parliament Building, Jose Fuste Raga; p 29 Geothermal Field, Peter Guttman; p 32 Lagos, Reuters; p 33 Victoria Falls, Roger De La Harpe, Gallo Images; p 42 Times Square, Jose Fuste Raga; p 43 Grand Canyon, James Randklev; p 48 Rio de Janeiro, Richard T. Nowitz; p 52 Tuvalu, Matthieu Paley; p 54 Inuit hunter, Layne Kennedy; p 55 Antarctic Research Base, Galen Rowell

Getty Images:
P 31 Alps, Altrendo Panoramic

Duncan McNeil:
P 13 Forth Road Bridge, D. McNeil, portrahere.me.uk.

MODIS Rapid Response Team, NASA/GSFC:
P 34 Nile Valley; p 38 The Gulf; p 46 Hurricane Katrina

Panos Pictures:
P 27 Moscow, Heldur Netocny

Science Photo Library:
P 21 UK Satellite image, p 24 Busy motorway

Mark Steward:
P 52 Sydney, p 53 Mount Cook

Still Pictures:
p 26 Mount Etna eruption, Otto Hahn; p 32 Giza, Malcolm S. Kirk; p 33 Sahara Desert, Frans Lemmens; p 35 Masai warriors, Friedrich Stark; p 36 Shanghai, Markus Dlouhy; p 49 Deforestation, S. Rocha-UNEP; p 53 Uluru, Raimund Franken

USGS EROS Data Centre:
P 37 Ganges Delta

Maps on the pages listed below are derived in part from material originally published in Collins Longman Atlases.
Keystart Junior Atlas:
P 26, pp 28-29, pp 30-31, p 32, p 36, p 42, p 48, p 52, pp 56-57

Acknowledgement
Editorial advisor: Dr. Stephen Scoffham